HEATH BOOKROOM

THE
Brookline
Trunk

T H E

Brookline Trunk

by LOUISE ANDREWS KENT

Illustrated by Barbara Cooney

APPLEWOOD BOOKS
Bedford, Massachusetts

Reprinted with the permission of
Houghton Mifflin Company.

Thank you for purchasing an Applewood book. Applewood
reprints America's lively classics—books from the past that
are still of interest to modern readers. For a free copy of our
current catalog, write to:

Applewood Books
P.O. Box 365
Bedford, MA 01730

ISBN: 1-55709-179-X

contents

Foreword

Dear Susie and Andrew:

At last our book about Brookline is finished!

It is often said that a happy country has no "history." This is true of towns too and Brookline is one of these happy towns. No great battle was ever fought here. The town has never had to rise from the ruins of a great fire or suffer through a flood, a plague, or a famine. No citizen of Brookline ever invented a hydrogen bomb or even, I am afraid, a plastic dog collar. Its inhabitants have been useful in many ways but they seldom make headlines in the newspapers. Two Presidents were born a few miles from here — but not in Brookline. Famous musicians have lived here but they always took care to be born somewhere else. Brookline likes art and artists but it imports them instead of growing them at home. People write an occasional book in Brookline, but the books are not the kind that shake empires. No one needs to be nervous about them.

Brookline does not have the highest building in the world or the biggest waterfall or the deepest canyon. It is, in fact, much like other American towns. It was a piece of wilderness. Men came here and won a living for themselves in spite of the wilderness. Some liked the place and stayed. Some of their children and grandchildren liked it and stayed too. Others thought the land looked better a little farther west.

Running through the town when the first settlers came was an old Indian trail. It was known for many years as the Old Sherburne Trail. Walnut Street is a piece of it. Heath Street is another. Gradually it was widened as ox teams plodded farther and farther from the sea. At last it was a road. People traveled as far as Framingham on it. There was talk of extending the road but a decision was made that it would not be necessary because "it was unlikely that white men would ever penetrate farther into the wilderness."

Yet in 1822 Mrs. Benjamin Goddard wrote to her niece in England, jokingly: "This will inform you that we are still hereabouts and not moved to the Ohio." The Ohio was a mysterious faraway place. Letters came back telling of a great river and of farm land very different from the rocky hillsides of New England. Brookline people moved toward it slowly. They measured the distance not in hours but in weeks of journeying, not in gallons of gasoline but in the sound of ripples against the side of a canal boat or in the slow thud of horses' feet on a muddy road. Somewhere beyond was always the wilderness. There were lakes like oceans, buffalo herds thundering across vast plains, painted savages, great ranges of mountains with snowy tops. To reach them meant crossing rivers so wide that the opposite shore might be lost in mist. Sometimes a traveler might think that he had reached that other ocean in the West. For, as time went on, people ceased to move away from the Atlantic. They were moving toward the Pacific.

The people who moved away and saw new places thought of Brookline as always the same. Yet it was changing all the time, and is still changing, no doubt, as I sit here writing this letter to you. While you were visiting me, you and I talked about the town and decided to write about it. Thank you for helping me. We aren't any of us historians and our book doesn't pretend to be a history. It is a book about the growth of an American town. It might be any town but it happens to be about Brookline and what it felt like to live there at different times during its first three centuries and part of a fourth one.

Most books about the growth of a place begin with the wilderness and work down to the present day. This one begins with the town as it is now and goes back to the wilderness. I chose this plan because I have noticed that if you want to find a road to a place you have never seen, you are not so likely to get lost if you start from a place you know already. That's why we have started with Brookline in 1955.

When we first talked about Brookline I said that we

would make our long journey backwards but that isn't exactly what we did. Our journey turns out to be a sort of shuttling. We go back every now and then about thirty years and see what Brookline was like at that time. We move forward in that period for a while, then make another backward jump. This one takes us even farther back in the life of the town, the next one farther still.

I have always liked an occasional look through the wrong end of my bird glasses. Everything gets smaller and smaller but so wonderfully clear — if I could only reach it. The glass through which we can look back into the past is through people's memories. If I tell you something my grandmother told me, that her grandmother told her, and that *she* learned from *her* grandmother, why, before we know it we are stepping out of a boat with the first little Puritan girl who ever set foot on the place she called Trimountain and that we call Boston.

Luckily, we've had help on our journey: from Miss Elizabeth Butcher, Librarian of the town, who suggested the book in the first place; from Miss Louise Rowley, the Children's Librarian, who encouraged us to think that if we wrote the book someone might read it; from Mrs. Bertram Little, who was most generous in sharing her knowledge with us. Her book on the Old Brookline Houses was especially helpful.

We are grateful, too, to people whom we shall never see

but whom we feel that we know from their letters and diaries, especially the members of the Goddard family. They not only had the admirable habit of writing letters and diaries but they kept them. Some of the diaries, letters, and account books come from our own family. It was your great-aunt, Katharine Andrews Frick, who reminded us of the story about the Jinitin Tree and then wrote it down for us to use. Your mother, Elizabeth Kent Gay, also wrote what she knew and remembered. The chapter called Friendly Town was written by her. This made her especially popular with

> *your grandmother,*
>
> LOUISE ANDREWS KENT

April 1955

To

my sister

KATHARINE

MARY

FRICK

1 9 5 5   Exploring With a Map   1

THIS IS HOW *The Brookline Trunk* happened to be written.

When Andrew and Susie came from Vermont to visit their grandmother in Brookline, she had lost her voice. This was unfortunate in a way. Of course there are advantages in having a grownup around who cannot talk but they had promised their teacher that they would write reports about Brookline and read them to the school when they got back to Kents' Corner. They had brought notebooks to write down things their grandmother told them about the way the town was managed. Now it looked as if she were not going to say anything except "Supper's ready," in a whisper.

"Grandma can't talk," Andrew wrote to their mother, "but she can still make strawberry shortcake. Wow! The taxi cost $1.75 and we gave the man fifteen cents. Forsythia is in blossom. There is no mud here. Tell Janet not to let Sparkle get muddy. She must clean him if she takes him out. Grandma likes the bracelet. She fastens it on with a piece of Scotch tape."

Sparkle Plenty — that was his whole name — was Andrew's black and white pony. Andrew had braided the bracelet out of hair from Sparkle's tail. Naturally his grandmother liked it.

Although the ground was dry in Brookline and anyway, as the children noticed, all the streets were paved and had sidewalks along them, it was Mud Time in Vermont. That meant big mudholes in the roads around Kents' Corner. It was so hard for many of the children to get to school that there was a Mud Time vacation. Several other boys and girls were going visiting too and they were all going to write reports about the places where they went.

Andrew and Susie told their grandmother that they were sorry she couldn't talk, because they wanted their reports to be especially good.

"You'll have to find out things for yourselves," she told them, whispering. "Now go to bed. In the morning we'll think up how you can do it. Good night."

"Good night, Grandma!" they whispered — because when one person whispers, everyone else does too.

The next morning Susie came downstairs early and got breakfast for herself and Andrew. Susie had started to learn to cook when she was so small that she had to stand on a chair to stir the scrambled eggs. Now that she was twelve she could make a great many good things. This morning she made an omelet and bacon. She fixed orange juice and cereal and milk and toast too. Afterwards she

rinsed off the dishes and put them in the dishwasher.
When her grandmother came downstairs, Susie was reading a book her great-great-great-grandfather had written
a hundred years ago and Andrew was reading a book written by his mother and grandmother more recently. There
was this habit of writing books in their family.

Mrs. Kent — that was their grandmother's name —
had a map in her hand. She had drawn it herself on a
rather large sheet of paper. It showed the streets in their
part of Brookline. She still had to whisper. She told
them that she could not take them out but they could
explore by themselves and mark things they found on the
map. The only thing she had marked on it besides the
names of the streets was her own house on Hawthorn
Road. She also gave them a list of things to find and put
down: "Two hospitals, a tennis court, at least one thing
you never saw before, at least one telephone and one
electric light pole, mailbox, fire alarm box. See how many
kinds of materials the houses are made of. Mark one of
each kind on the map. What would you like for dinner?"

"Chicken pie," Andrew said. "String beans," Susie
said. "Gingerbread with marshmallows," Andrew said.
"Mushrooms with the string beans and inside-out-pota-
toes," Susie said.

"You've thought of enough," their grandmother whispered.

Luckily she had most of the things ready in the freezer,
as her grandchildren well knew. She cooked things ahead
of time and froze them for just such emergencies. In fact
all she had to cook now was the potatoes.

The frozen food was thawed out when the explorers came back. They had found everything on the list. They had numbered the different things and put corresponding numbers on the map.

"There's almost nothing on the list that we have in Kents' Corner," Andrew said as he finished his second helping of chicken pie. "The houses are certainly very different from the ones at home. Ours are almost all covered with clapboards and painted white. And the barns are red with white trimmings. I think they are pretty. But, of course," he added politely, "these houses are very *interesting*. So many colors — gray and yellow and green. I even saw a pink one with blue shutters. How many things did we count that they were built of, Susie?"

"Stone, bricks of different colors. Imitation brick siding — that's what you hate, isn't it, Grandma?"

His grandmother said "Ugh!" — as much as she could make this noise in a whisper — and Susie went on: "Something that we think is plaster — some rough and some smooth. Shingles. Big beams with plaster in between. And mixtures — brick and wood, stone and wood, stone and brick."

"Write all these things down before you forget them," their grandmother whispered. "I'll think what you had better do tomorrow."

The next morning they started out again with the map. This time they went down the hill to the village. They had already noticed that the one thing about Brookline that was a little like their own village was the hills. They were much smaller, of course, than Vermont hills but there were plenty of them. Their grandmother, whose voice was a little better, told them that like hills everywhere a good many of them were named after early settlers. There were Fisher Hill, Aspinwall Hill, Corey Hill, and Heath Hill. Streets had names of the first settlers too — Boylston Street, Griggs Road, Sewall Avenue, Gardner Road. The hill they walked down, however, did not have a family name. Instead it had two names. It was called High Street Hill by the world in general because High Street ran over it. Its private name was Pill Hill because of the many doctors who liked to live there. They could be near Boston hospitals and still enjoy living where there were grass and trees and flowers.

It was an old-fashioned part of town, their grandmother told the children, and had not changed much since she was a little girl. There were the same big ugly comfortable houses, cool in summer, warm in winter. Only this year they had taken down the iron lampposts on Hawthorn Road. The gas had been burning dimly in them as long as she could remember. The same magnolias and forsythias had been blooming every spring for more than half a century. Sometimes it seemed as if the same children were playing hopscotch on the same sidewalks.

Perhaps, she said, Andrew and Susie would rather play hopscotch than go to the village.

They would rather go to the village, they said, and mark some more things on the map.

The first thing their grandmother had written on the list was Fire Station. They found it very easily at the bottom of the hill, right on Route 9.

"This must be Boylston Street, the one Grandma said you could go to New York on," Susie said, marking it on the map.

"Looks like a long walk," Andrew said. "Hey, don't these cars ever stop?"

They wanted to cross Boylston Street so they could get a better look at the Fire Station, a big brick building with a clock tower. Would the traffic lights never be right? Their grandmother had told them not to cross except when the lights were red and yellow. A great stream of cars — enormous trailer trucks, buses that stopped with a swishing sound, nimble little sport cars, jeeps, station wagons, Cadillacs with chauffeurs in peaked caps — seemed to move on forever. Then suddenly all the lights flashed red. The traffic stopped, the doors of the fire station opened, a siren sounded, and out came the biggest fire engine the children had ever seen. It was just what a fire engine ought to be: red and gold, gleaming with polished metal, with long ladders shining like silver, and flashing lights like rubies.

The firemen were putting on their coats and helmets as the engine turned up Washington Street. Another smaller engine and the chief's big car went past much too fast for the children to see how they looked. All three soon disappeared, but the noise of the sirens sounded in the distance for some time. Then the traffic lights on Route 9 turned green again and the river of cars roared on. By this time there were several people waiting to cross. After a minute one of the men pushed a button on the traffic-light pole. The lights turned red and yellow, brakes squealed, cars stopped, and everyone could cross the street.

Andrew and Susie zipped across, passed the Savings Bank, and started along Washington Street. Going over the railroad bridge, Susie said, "Wait, Andrew! Look — we're in luck — a train is coming!"

It was only a short train, the cars were old and dingy, and the engine had seen better days. Still it made a satisfactory amount of noise as it rattled along under the bridge and slammed to a stop at the station. Susie marked the bridge on the map. "Come on, Andrew. Paine's is on this side of the street. I remember where it is."

"Zowie!" Andrew said, "only I don't have much money."

"They don't mind your looking if you don't handle things. We'll tell the ladies that we are going to decide later what we'll buy. They are friends of mine."

There were so many wonderful things at Paine's that they could not make up their minds what to buy for their mother and Janet and Olivia. They decided to think it over and come back the next day. They also went into the Five and Ten, which had been all fixed over into a serve-yourself store like a supermarket with carriages to push. Andrew bought a goldfish and a bowl to put it in for his grandmother. He had earned the money himself by selling bantam eggs to his mother. Susie went into Barnaby's next door and bought a yellow rosebud for the living room mantelpiece. Her grandmother was very much pleased, of course, and she enjoyed hearing about the new things they had seen.

Susie and Andrew had added several things to their list — things they did not have in their own village: police cars that drove around the streets with DRIVE SAFELY or SAFETY FIRST painted on the back and with loudspeakers on top, a policeman collecting pennies and nickels from parking meters, another one holding up traffic for them as they crossed Harvard Street. The list was getting longer and longer. There was a drinking fountain. Andrew had a drink out of it by pressing something that made the water bubble up. There were the orange-colored buses, the train, and the white lines painted along the streets. There was the clock in the church tower, a flock of pigeons wheeling through the air, a great flight of jet planes thundering above them, and the big overpass that carried the traffic of Route 1 over Route 9. There was the traffic circle beautifully planted with tulips and flowering shrubs and the roar of the trolley cars from across Muddy River.

That afternoon their grandmother told them — still in a whisper — how to find the Wishing Stone. They were to walk up Walnut Street, the oldest in Brookline, once an Indian trail through a dark forest, until they came to a triangle of land where they would see a bronze tablet on a stone marker. This was the center of the town, she told them. Near it used to stand the first meeting-house and the first schoolhouse. The big stone church with the square tower was a descendant of the first meeting house and the gray stone part of it close to the street was Brookline's first town hall and a schoolhouse besides. It was called Pierce Hall, she said, and from there she told them how to find the Wishing Stone. It's a secret of hers and she never tells it much above a whisper even when she can talk all right and then only to just the right person at the right time.

"How did you find out about it?" Susie asked.

"From my mother, who used to wish on it and who showed me how. And she learned about it from her mother. Now when you find it, you lick your thumb and press it against the little red stone — it looks like a piece of sealing wax — shut your eyes, hold your breath, and wish HARD. And don't tell what you wish."

"This has been done," she added, "by so many generations of Brookline children that the stone is getting rather worn and shabby looking. Still I don't believe it has lost its power."

"Did you ever get anything you wished for?" Susie asked.

"I got a bicycle, a pair of beaded bronze slippers, and a college education," their grandmother replied.

"Did you tell anyone what you wished?" Andrew asked.

His grandmother turned a chuckle into a slight cough and answered, "Not afterwards."

"You mean, you told before?" Susie asked.

"I sometimes took that precaution," the grandmother admitted.

They found the bronze tablet and read how the men of Brookline met on the triangle on the morning of the nineteenth of April in 1775 and marched to Lexington. Then they hunted for the Wishing Stone and found it, just where their grandmother had said it would be. They wished on it as she had told them to do. On the way home they stopped and read the names of their ancestors on the stones in the quiet graveyard. They found the place on the map where their grandmother had marked GARRISON HOUSE. It was near the corner of Walnut and Chestnut Streets across from the graveyard.

"I wish it were there still and we could fight Indians from it," Andrew said.

"I don't," said Susie. "Anyway Grandma said Brookline people didn't fight Indians. That they were friends."

"What did they have a garrison house for then?"

"I don't know. We'll have to ask her when her voice is better."

Farther down the street they found the house where their grandmother was born.

"No bronze tablet on it," Andrew told her when they got home.

"Well anyway not *yet*," Susie said politely.

Susie wrote to her mother that night. "Grandma can almost talk now. She is going to drive us out exploring tomorrow if it's a good day. We went down to Leverett's Pond and fed the ducks just the way you used to. We saw the Lawrence School. We didn't know it would be so big. Grandma says she went there, only this is a new building. We wish we could go for a few days just to see what it's like. Only we are like the ducks and we really belong in the north. We'll be coming home in a few days now. Please give my love to Janet and O.

SUSIE"

THE NEXT DAY there was snow on the forsythias and a cold wind. Later the snow changed to a rain like icicles that were melted — but not enough.

"I suppose you can't take us exploring," Andrew said.

"No, but you can go by yourselves," said his grandmother, "right in this house."

"When? How? What for? Where?" both children asked as fast as they could speak.

"Anywhere in the house except not in any bureau or closet drawers. The thing you are looking for is too big to go in a drawer. You can arrange with each other how — whether you'll go together or each choose different places. I don't think it will take you many days. Of course I can supply you with explorers' rations — pemmican or that package of K-ration your Uncle Sam brought home from Italy when he left the army. Or would you rather come back for lunch?"

"Back!" they both said.

"Good. I shall be delighted to see you. You are to hunt for a small trunk covered with brown leather. It's about twenty inches long and fourteen inches wide. It has a curved top and a design in brass-headed nails on it. It's lined with an old wallpaper. You can decide whether the pattern is seaweed or feathers. On top of the lid is a brass handle something like the ones on the highboy in the dining room."

"What's in it?" Andrew asked.

"That's what you are going to find out."

"O.K.!" they said. "When do we start?"

"Why, now," said their grandmother, who was melting up a quarter of a pound of butter for a pan of brownies.

"Come on, Andrew, let's try the closet under the stairs first. It has about everything in it."

The closet under the stairs did indeed contain an interesting collection of objects. There were electric light bulbs, old Christmas cards, overshoes, tennis racquets, candlesticks, a copper jug with garden tools in it, and an outfit for playing miniature golf.

"No trunks," said Andrew, "I guess we'd better try the cellar."

The cellar had some trunks in it but they were too big and they were all locked. There was no small brown one among the rakes and hoes and spades and skis. No trunk on the shelf with the cans of maple syrup or in the old coal bin where there were still a few dusty looking lumps of coal left over when the gas furnace was put in.

"Let's try some closets upstairs," Susie said.

The upstairs closets were very uninteresting — tailored suits in plastic bags, transparent hatboxes and shoe bags full of shoes. In one closet there were shelves piled with linen, smelling of rose leaves and lavender. Another had the vacuum cleaner in it and smelled of floor wax. Still another had a full shelf of bound volumes of *The Youth's Companion*. No trunk.

Susie would have stopped to see if she could find any of the stories her grandfather used to write for *The Companion* but Andrew made her go on. He said they had to look under all the beds. They did — and under all the sofas too: still no trunk.

"We are wasting our time," Andrew said. "Let's try the attic."

The attic was dimly lighted by a skylight and one electric bulb. There were shadowy corners with strange shapes looming out of them. It was a well-furnished attic. Squirrly-legged tables had queer old lamps on them. A printing press and a big box of type were next to a washbowl and pitcher painted with pink daisies. There was one trunk but it was big and covered with black leather. It had a tag on it that said RIDING CLOTHES. They thought the small trunk might be in it so they took the clothes out — coats and skirts of black broadcloth, breeches and long coats of linen, a coat and breeches of green corduroy, a tweed coat and jodhpurs.

While they were putting the clothes back, they saw the door. It was just behind the trunk and big enough to go through on their hands and knees. It was open a little way so they could look in. Susie said, "See, Andrew — it's like Grandma's house in Kents' Corner. We can crawl in."

They did, feeling around them as they went and sneezing occasionally.

"I've found something," Andrew announced. "It feels — kerchoo — like a sword."

"Good for you. As for me, I've found the trunk! It's leathery and I can feel the brass handle and the nails."

"Fine — kerchoo — let's back out," said Andrew.

It was a rather dusty pair of explorers who emerged into what now seemed like a brightly lighted attic, dragging the sword in its crumbling leather sheath and the small brown trunk with its curved top and tarnished brasses. It was locked and it felt heavy for its size. They carried it carefully downstairs. Andrew nearly tripped over the sword, which came almost up to his shoulder. It was not made for anyone ten years old. They arrived in the kitchen right side up just as their grandmother was taking the brownies out of the pan.

They both talked very fast, telling how they found the trunk.

"I believe," said Susie, "that someone pushed it in with the sword and left them both. Grandma, you look very twinkly — did you do it?"

"Well, yes," her grandmother said.

"When? When? Years ago?"

"Not so very long ago — last night when it began to snow, actually. And I must say I thought you'd take longer to find it. I figured I'd have lunch ready before you came back. But the chicken is in the electric roaster and we have time to see what's in the trunk before the time bell rings. Shall we open it? I have the key in my pocket."

"Yes, yes — right away!"

"Let's take it into the living room where we can spread things out. You carry it, Susie. Now you mustn't be disappointed. There's no gold or silver or diamonds or maps about buried treasure in it. Still, there's a kind of treasure — it has more than three hundred years of Brookline in it."

"Why, there is too some gold," Andrew said as his grandmother turned the key in the lock and opened the lid.

So there was — stamped on the covers of diaries, on the cases of daguerreotypes, on the back of a thick book called *Muddy River Records 1634–1833*. There were silhouettes too, framed in something that looked like gold but, their grandmother said, was really thin brass. There were gold threads in an old piece of brocade. If there were no emeralds or rubies or sapphires, at least there were scraps of old dresses in all these colors. Silver buckles gleamed on a small pair of white satin slippers. So there was silver, as Andrew did not fail to point out. The seaweed pattern on the paper lining of the trunk was silvery white against a background of dandelion gold. An old pocketbook was embroidered in every color of the rainbow and a few extra ones besides. A broken saucer with a clipper ship in full sail on it had a blue border with gold stars.

Susie loved all these things but Andrew was more in-

terested in drawings showing some old Brookline houses,
letters with old stamps on them, and an Indian arrowhead. Most of the other things, he said, were sissy — a
favorite word of his.

"So you think these are sissy?" his grandmother asked
picking up the embroidered pocketbook and a piece of
faded red flannel. "Perhaps you may change your mind
when I tell you about them."

"I want to hear a story about everything in the trunk,"
Susie said.

"So do I," Andrew said, "especially the arrowhead.
Isn't that your handwriting in that red book? Have you
written about them?"

His grandmother said that she had started to write
something but that she had not finished.

"Please do the rest and read it all to us," said Susie.

"I'm afraid there isn't time — you have to go home so
soon. But perhaps I can tell you some things now, and
more when I see you in the summer."

"Were you going to write a book?" asked Andrew.

Their grandmother said that she had had some such
idea but that it was always quite a lot easier not to write
a book than to write one.

"You might write about what it was like to live in
Brookline all the way back to when some Indian shot this
arrowhead," Andrew said. "I mean what it was like to
be a boy, of course."

"AND a girl," Susie added. "Perhaps Mother would
help. She might write about when she was a girl in
Brookline and you might write what you remember and

things your mother and grandmother told you. And you
could find out about other people from some of these
letters, couldn't you?"

"Well, I could try," said their grandmother.
So she did.

THE LAST EVENING of their visit had come and they
were busy packing the presents they had bought for the
family when the telephone rang. They heard their grandmother say, "Oh NO! . . . Well, I'm glad it's no worse . . .
How are *you?* . . . Gracious! . . . Of course — as long as
you like . . . School . . . I expect I can arrange it . . . "

By this time, of course, both children were breathing
down her neck so she added, "They'd like to speak to
you. Take this telephone, Susie. Andrew, you scuttle
upstairs and use the one there . . . Yes, it's your mother."

So then they heard the news from Kents' Corner. Janet
had scarlet fever and Olivia had whooping cough.

"And how are you, Mother?" they both asked at once.

"I," said their mother, "have both."

She added that they were not any of them very sick,
thanks to some miracle drugs with long names, but they

were all in quarantine so Andrew and Susie couldn't come home. Perhaps they could get their wish and go to the Lawrence School, she said.

"It isn't a very nice way to get my wish," Susie said. "I wish I'd never *touched* that old wishing stone!"

Her mother began to laugh and that made her cough and the conversation came to an end.

On Monday they started going to their grandmother's old school. It seemed strange at first because there were so many children and there seemed to be miles of corridors. At Kents' Corner the whole school was in one room of the white wooden schoolhouse. In this fine brick building Susie was in the seventh grade and Andrew in the sixth and they hardly ever saw each other. However, they soon began to feel at home, to know their way around the building, and to know some of the other boys and girls.

While Susie and Andrew were in school their grandmother was working on her book. In the evenings she would tell them things she had learned. Sometimes she had written something and she would read it to them.

I am writing the book backwards, she told them. Most books about towns or cities begin as far back as you can go and gradually work down to the kind of world we know. I think it might be interesting for a change, she said, to begin with the town the way it is now and then look back at it every twenty-five or thirty years and see how it changes and why and what it was like to live there. Do you think that would be a good plan in trying to learn how a town grows?

"Well," said Andrew, "it seems a little like standing on your head while you walk downstairs but it's all right with me. There's one thing I'd like to ask you before you start. Why do you keep calling it a town? It seems more like a city to me."

"Yes," said Susie, "all those fire engines and the police cars and the big High School, all those other schools, the gymnasium — it really is practically a city, isn't it?"

Their grandmother said that they were perfectly right. Brookline had more than fifty thousand people living in it. Nearer sixty than fifty, really. That is more than there are in any Vermont city, more than there are in a great many cities all through the United States.

"Why does it pretend to be a town then? Is it so people will say it's the richest town in the world?" Andrew asked. "Is it run just like a town?"

For a long time, she told him, Brookline was managed like any New England town. When things had to be decided about schools or streets or the library, people met in the Town Hall, chose a moderator, talked things over and voted what to do. They elected selectmen and other town officers and the selectmen carried out the decisions of the meeting. This system worked very well until about the beginning of this century. By that time there were so many voters that they could not all possibly get into the Town Hall. Sometimes it happened that all the people who were in favor of something or who opposed something — perhaps a new firehouse or a school building — would pack the hall so full that those who were on the other side could neither speak nor vote.

In 1915 the town decided on a new plan called the Limited Town Meeting. Brookline is now divided into twelve precincts. The voters of each precinct elect twenty-seven representatives. These representatives with some of the town officers, who are called representatives-at-large, make up the Limited Town Meeting. They meet and carry on the business of the town but any citizen may go to the meeting, listen to the discussions, and speak on the subject being discussed. There are still five selectmen to carry out the decisions of the meeting. Heads of the different departments — school, library, welfare, recreation, public health, water, police, fire — report to the meeting.

Like other towns Brookline has a Town Treasurer to handle the town's money and a Town Clerk to take care of the records. All towns have the same kinds of problems. Brookline has more people in it so it has to do things on a larger scale than a smaller place does. There have to be more desks in the schoolrooms, more miles of streets and water pipes, more books in the library, more parking meters along the streets.

As for this "richest town in the world" business, she added, I don't think that Brookline people take that very seriously. I don't know if it is even so and anyway it never meant that all Brookline people were rich. It only meant that the value of the houses and land in Brookline was high — for a town. It didn't mean that we have grand marble buildings like Washington, or a wonderful Art Museum like Chicago, theaters like New York, restaurants known all over the world like New Orleans, or magnificent shops like Dallas or Los Angeles.

Still it's comfortable — at least I think so. I heard someone say once that civilization was the art of living comfortably together in large numbers. Perhaps that makes Brookline count as a civilized place. Most of its people live where they can see grass and trees growing. Ever since I can remember there has been a tree-planting committee to be sure that every new street in town has trees planted along it. If an old tree falls in a hurricane, a new one is planted to take its place. I have a long list of the different kinds of trees in town. I'll show it to you sometime. Long before most towns thought about town planning, Brookline had a Planning Board to decide where shops could be built, and how far houses must be set back from the street, and what space to save for playgrounds. It is no accident that the traffic circles are attractive to look at as you wait your turn to edge around them in a crowded hour. Tulips save tempers, I always think at such times. It took many years of planning before everyone in town could have pure, clear water just by turning a tap.

We are likely to take such things for granted but we ought to be both proud of them and grateful for them — for streets that are clean all the year round, for good schools for everyone, for a library where you can read and look at fine pictures and listen to music, for efficient police and fire departments to protect our property.

"Have you lived here all your life?" asked Andrew.

"Not yet," said his grandmother. "Only since May 25th, 1886."

I think it's fair to say — she went on — that it's a pleasant civilized place to live. It's really a rich town in ways that count but it's rich because of where it happens to be — surrounded on three sides by a great city. You know how many times when we are driving I tell you, "We're in Boston now," and then in a few minutes we'll be back in Brookline again. If we could pick Brookline up and set it down in the lovely green hills of Vermont, it would be — with its fifty-seven thousand people and its one hundred miles of paved streets and its more than a hundred miles of water pipes — the largest city in the state. Only it couldn't keep alive for a week. A city can't live without industry. Brookline has hardly any but it has Boston. Its citizens sleep comfortably in Brookline. Most of them earn their living in Boston.

When we went to the Zoo and the Museum of Science and the Airport, we went to Boston. When you go to England this summer, Susie, you won't have much luck taking ship on the Muddy River but you can sail from Boston. Your train home goes from Boston — not Brookline. The Arboretum, where we went to see the cherry trees in bloom, is in Boston. So are the swanboats, Andrew, and those wonderful Chinese paintings you liked so much, Susie. That shining gold dome above Boston Common belongs to Brookline people but no more than to any other citizens of the commonwealth. When we watch the lights on the John Hancock tower to see what the weather is going to do, we are looking into Boston.

If you wanted to buy a bale of cotton to make some sheets or wool to weave blankets or leather to make shoes or a ton of tea, you'd find them in Boston. People come from all over the world to consult Boston doctors. Students from every state in the union and from many foreign countries come to Boston or across the river to Cambridge to study. Brookline gets its gas and electricity from Boston. Even its milk, some of which comes from Kents' Corner, gets to Brookline by way of Boston.

I could keep this up — she said — for the rest of the evening — but perhaps by this time you are wondering what Brookline has to offer anyway. Well, it has what any good town has — fine men in its churches, devoted teachers in its school rooms, honest, sensible, efficient town officers, and good neighbors on every street. It may be just a bedroom for Boston but it's a pretty good one — and speaking of bedrooms . . .

"Good night," they said. "Good night."

We haven't talked much about the trunk yet," Susie said the next evening.

She had been reading a letter from her mother. Janet and Olivia had exchanged diseases but no one was very sick. They had been making popcorn, she said.

It is a good evening for popcorn here too — her grandmother said — so Susie and Andrew had a competition. It was chilly and they had a fire going. Susie popped hers over the fire in an old-fashioned wire corn popper. Andrew, always in favor of modern methods, did his in the kitchen by electricity. His grandmother, when called on to judge the results, admired Andrew's batch because every grain was perfect. However, she said, she really liked Susie's better. It was so buttery and the slightly scorched taste and the half-popped grains seemed more homelike somehow.

After they had unbuttered themselves, Susie wrote a letter to her mother.

"Thank you for your letter," she wrote. "I never had a letter that was fumigated before. We have been making popcorn like O. and J. Grandma is very old-fashioned. She has never been in an airplane! Can you imagine that? She wears a hat when she goes to the village and she likes her popcorn scorched. As soon as I finish this she is going to read us something out of your journal. She says you told her it was all right to. It was in The Brookline Trunk. That's what we call the trunk where she keeps her old historic papers. She is going to tell us about something that's in the trunk every night. She has the things all arranged with the newest ones on top and the oldest at the bottom. She says we are going to jump back thirty years and see what Brookline was like when you were my age. Your journal is on top of the pile and she is going to read to us out of it. Andrew is putting together a Model T Ford. Grandma says it is like her first car. I have a new paintbrush and paper and Chinese ink. I am going to try to make a picture like some I saw at the Museum. If one turns out well, I am going to have it framed for Grandma for her birthday. Andrew is making the Model T for her. When I get my pictures done, I think I will start writing a journal for my children."

So while Susie worked on her picture and Andrew put a brass band around the radiator of the Ford, their grandmother read to them out of their mother's journal.

Brookline, 1925. My godfather gave me this notebook for Christmas. He told me that now that I am 12 years old I should keep a journal. A journal is different from a diary. A diary just tells that you get up in the morning and go to school and maybe to dancing school or to a party, what they had to eat, etc., if it snowed or rained. It is not very interesting to write or to read even if it does have a lock and key.

The journal has no dates in it. It has a red leather cover with gold leaves around the edge. My godfather says that when I have filled it up he will get me another one. I can write anything I like in it.

First I will tell about myself and then about where I live, in case I want to read about those things when I am old.

My name is Elizabeth but I am called Bunny at home and Kenty at school. My hair is absolutely straight and cut across in bangs like Buster Brown. I used to wish for curls but now I don't care any more. My hair is brown and so are my eyes and I am not pretty. I like to climb trees and ride my bicycle and make up stories and act in plays and to read books and play with my friends.

I live in the house where I was born, very near Brookline Village, just across from Emerson Park. It is built of gray clapboards with white trimmings and green doors and shutters. My room is over the front door and from my bed I can look out into the street and across to the park. I can see everyone and everything that goes by.

In the mornings quite a few fathers walk down the street on their way to work in Boston. Mine is one of

them. They walk through the park with their briefcases
and down to the station where they take the train to work.
Or they take a streetcar on Washington Street and go
down to the Transfer Station. The railroad track runs
close enough to the house so that we hear the trains and
see their smoke. There is a footbridge over the tracks off
White Place. Sometimes my brother — his name is Hol-
lister, but everyone calls him Sam, for some reason — and
I go down to watch the trains. They come through quite
slowly as they have just left the station and they make a
lot of noise and smoke, puffing and rattling along to the
next stop at Brookline Hills.

A little later the fathers go to work who have shops or
offices in the village, or who work at the Town Hall. Firemen and policemen and constables all live on our street.
I see them go by in their uniforms and sometimes they
come home to lunch. When we walk down to the village
we often see them again. The firemen will be sitting near
the door of the firehouse or polishing the big engine or
answering a fire alarm. The policemen direct traffic or
walk their beats. If we go into the Town Hall there are
quite a few people we know in the different offices.

Right behind our house lives one of the mailmen who
delivers mail from the post office. His two daughters are
some of my best friends. One of the first things I remember is running away down the garden to play with them.
It was after I had gone to bed and I had on my nightgown.
I had a new pair of red slippers that I wanted to show
them. The mailman's brother also works at the post office.
He sells stamps at one of the windows. He tells Mother

about books he is reading. His favorite author is Ralph Waldo Emerson.

Although our street is quiet, it is never dull. Some kind of wagon or truck is always passing by. There are more automobiles than horses but the milkman still has a horse. He comes so early in the morning that mostly I don't see him. I just hear him whistling and hear the rattle of the milk bottles in the rack. His horse knows all the stops because for years he has been going to the same houses on the same route. In winter he comes in a pung with jingling sleigh bells. We don't have any horses now but we have two cars. The other day my father had a portable garage put up for them in the back yard. Mother started making a chocolate pudding just when the men came and they finished the garage before she finished the pudding.

Some mornings the street department trucks come around. The garbage men are always whistling, too, and I hear the lids of the garbage cans in the back of the house crash shut and then the truck moving along the street. Or they might be picking up trash from the cans along the sidewalk or loads of ashes.

Other trucks come and clean up the branches after a big storm, or spray the trees against beetles. Every so often men come to mend the street. The tar truck comes with its sharp hot smell and then the steamroller. And of course in the winter they plow the snow into great piles beside the sidewalks and in front of people's houses, higher than my head, so high that my brother and I often dig caves in them that we can sit in.

Just across the street from my window is a tall lamp-

post. The lamp is very high above the street and at night
it makes a strange hissing and buzzing sound. Once in a
while boys throw stones and break it and then a special
truck has to come with very high ladders and put on a new
globe.

As I lie in bed I can look right at the lamp and it is a
friendly sight. All along the street are smaller lampposts
and the lamplighter comes to light them every evening.
They make a different sort of sound, more of a whisper.
We often follow him along the sidewalk and watch him
reach up into the lamp with his long tool and turn up the
light. He knows us and waves to us when he goes away.

The scissors grinder knows us too. He comes with the
big grinder on his back and people bring out their knives
and scissors to him to be sharpened. In the spring comes
the balloon man with all colors of balloons floating over
his head and all the children run to buy them. The organ
grinder comes with his music box slung across his shoulders. He brings it round in front of him, lets down a leg
for it to stand on, and grinds away. The front of the box
is painted with Italian lakes and mountains and the music
rolls out loud and clear. Afterwards his monkey in a red
jacket goes round offering his hat for pennies.

In the spring, too, we see Italian women in their long
black dresses digging for dandelion greens in the park
with their sharp little knives. Their aprons are full of
greens by the end of the day. They must come from far
off as we don't see them any other time. The keeper of
the park goes round with his trash can on wheels and
keeps the park tidy. Once a man came with a set of bag-

pipes and played and played. We gave him our pennies. Another time a man came with two ponies. We could have a ride and our photograph taken for a dollar. Mother let us do it and we rode around the park.

Sometimes it seems that we live more in the park than we do at home. It is a half-moon of grass with gravel walks around the edge and tall shrubs and trees next to the high iron railings. There are benches to sit down on and in one corner there are some sandboxes and a drinking fountain.

I like the park best when I have it all to myself. In the spring I find the first dandelions there and in the fall I get up early, early in the morning to run across and pick up the horse chestnuts that have fallen during the night. Down come the rough green cases when the nuts are ripe and out spill the glossy red-brown chestnuts. They're not good to eat, but they are fun to cut up and make rings and baskets and dolls' dishes, and to tie to a string and play different games with. One boy will hit his chestnut against another boy's and see which one breaks.

We don't roller-skate in the park because it isn't paved. We do that on the sidewalk. We also play jackstones on the sidewalk in the spring, mark out hopscotch with chalk, skip rope, and bounce balls.

Our block has a lot of different things on it, not just people's houses. Once I ran away around the block. I wanted to see what was on the other side. I ran up the street past the house with the Pomeranians, past the constable's, past a boardinghouse, round the corner onto Cypress Street. Then I ran along to Washington Street where there was a little collection of stores on the corner opposite the library. I remember most a store where we got our first Eskimo Pies. Down along this next stretch I would have come to the fire station on the corner of Thayer Street but I think they caught me before that. I must have been two or even less.

Another thing I remember long ago is going with my mother to see the statue being brought on a great wagon to be placed on the grass by the library. We watched the men put it in place and then we came again to see it unveiled. And I remember hearing a great sound of bells and whistles and running over to the fire station to see what it was. It was the false armistice of the First World War, and the firemen were sitting on top of the engine in the firehouse and clanging the big bells and shouting. My mother had just got off her horse and had on her green riding coat and breeches. She and I both ran down the street pushing Sam in his carriage. In a few days more it was the real armistice and the bells rang all day.

I like to go to the livery stable opposite the Town Hall. I watch the wagons go in and out and see the huge loads of hay being put into the loft. A fork is let down and fastened into the bale of hay and then drawn up and swung into the loft with a great rattle and clatter. Mr. Goodspeed who owns the livery stable lives on our street, just the other side of the tall street light and his daughter and I play together in her yard or mine most of the time.

Across the street in the other direction lives Mr. Paine who keeps the nicest store in the village. Whenever we have a present to buy we always go to Paine's. Besides toys of every kind they have all sorts of stationery, books, and magazines. Everyone in the store is very kind and they let you look and look a long time before you choose what you want. ("Just like now!" said Susie.) Paine's is also the newspaper store and every morning and evening it is full of noise and excitement at the side door where the trucks bring the papers and the newsboys collect the ones they are going to deliver.

Down the street from Paine's is Mackey's. It is the hardware store where we buy tools and garden things, new teakettles and nails. Soon after that, is Young and Brown's, the drugstore where we get our ice cream on Sundays, cough drops and prescriptions, cologne and adhesive tape. Farther along still is the Women's Exchange where the best cakes and cookies and jelly come from.

When we cross over and come up the other side we come to Peter's shoe store. In the spring we get our new sneakers there and in the fall our school shoes and our patent leathers for dancing school. Farther up the block is Delano's which sells thread and cloth and notions of all sorts. The bank and the 5 & 10 are on the next block.

The biggest store of all is Rhodes Brothers which stands at the head of the open space where Harvard Street and Washington Street come together. I can't imagine a kind of food that can't be bought in that store. Near the front are the breads and cakes. Over on the left are the deep bins for the different sorts of sugar and the bright red coffee cans and the tall grinder. At the back stand the butcher and the fishman at their counters and chopping blocks. Far back on the left is a wide, low doorway with wires strung across it on which slide metal plates with numbers that call the various salesmen to the front of the store.

No. 4 has been our salesman for as long as I can remember. He wears a long white coat and a cap in winter and a straw hat in summer. When we were little, he used to lift us up to sit on the high counter where he does his wrapping and figuring. His pencil is behind his ear and his order book in his hand and he never walks but always seems to run a little.

At the back where the salesmen have their counter is also the place where the orders are made up and put into heavy wicker baskets and slid through to the wagons. You can hear the horses stamping, the wheels shifting on

the pavement, and the drivers shouting while the wagons
are being filled with deliveries.

Even when I was quite small, I was sent down to get
groceries at Rhodes so I learned my way to No. 4's desk
very soon. I also knew my way to the other stores in the
village about as soon as I could read. I would fetch butter
and eggs from Morgan's and watch them slice the butter
from the big tubs and choose the eggs from the different
baskets. And then have an ice-cream cone from the
change. They are cake cones and cost 3 cents and the
pineapple sherbert is the best.

I went to Delano's for spools of thread for the dress-
maker who came every week to our house to make our
clothes, down to Young & Brown's for a prescription, over
to Paine's for a block of paper and home again past the bicycle shop and the Town Hall.

One good thing in our town is the trees. Another is
plenty of walls to walk on.

The best wall is at the library. About as early as I
remember anything I remember my father taking me to
the library on Saturday afternoon or Sunday just so I
could walk on the walls there and run up and down the
steps in front. The first painting I ever noticed more
than once was a picture of the sea with wild blue-green
waves dashing at some rocks. First it was in Mr. Fitzgerald's gallery. Later it hung in the hallway of the
library.

Mr. Fitzgerald's gallery was on Washington Street.
Mother used to take me there to see the pictures. Many
of them were by French painters, he told us. The gallery

was attached to his house. It seemed to be full of light, not only from the lights overhead but from within the paintings. They glowed with sunshine. The gallery was very big, but there wasn't room for all his pictures. He had so many prints and drawings that he kept boxes of them under his bed, he told us.

Among the trees I am most fond of I have told about the big horse chestnut in the park already. Another is a big copper beech on Davis Avenue. It is so tall and its branches hang down so close to the ground that we can play underneath as though it was a great tent. Next to our house stands a tall elm whose branches brush the windows. In summer they make a soft swishing whisper and in winter the twigs tap and click or rattle with a coating of ice.

Every year we go to visit the Arboretum, which is on the other side of the town. We go when the forsythia is out and when the cherry trees are in bloom and later when the lilacs are in bloom. We also drive through the Sargent estate in the spring to see the flowering trees. We walk around Ward's Pond and watch for a big orange goldfish or go down to Muddy River to feed the mallards and to see whether the wood duck with his brightly colored head and wings has come back. We walk around the old Brookline reservoir and in winter we skate there.

The nineteenth of April is a special sort of holiday in Brookline because then we go up to Washington Street to watch William Dawes ride by on his way to Lexington. The real William Dawes rode this way from Boston to warn the colonists that the British were coming. Dr. Joseph Warren sent both Dawes and Paul Revere to carry the news. Revere crossed the Charles River. Dawes got out of the city when the British soldiers were changing the guard and rode through Roxbury and Brookline.

After lunch on the nineteenth we go over to Beacon Street to see the first runners in the Marathon come wearily down the street. Mostly it is Clarence DeMar who wins.

Almost every year we go to the Children's Museum at Jamaica Plain. I like the stuffed birds and the Japanese house there. We also don't have far to go to the Museum of Fine Arts. There we like to look at the Egyptian collection with models of men and boats and the Greek vases and statues. After we come home we play that we are Egyptians for quite a while.

The Zoo at Franklin Park is also near, so we go there several times a year. We know best the bird house, the elephants called Molly, Waddy, and Tony, the lions and tigers and the monkeys. If only the cages would not smell so!

In winter we go coasting on what Sam calls the High Hill. It is really just the steep bank at the far end of the land that faces the High School. It is a very popular place to coast and on good winter afternoons it is hard to see the snow for sleds and children. Over beyond the bank the big boys skate and play hockey. Sometimes we go swimming at the Municipal Baths. On the way home we look in at the door of the blacksmith's by the bridge. We

sniff the smell of scorching hooves and hot iron and watch
the sparks fly at the forge while the shoes are being ham-
mered out.

I've told about running along the walls at the Library
but, of course, now we are bigger, we go inside and read
the books. At first Mother took them out for us and later
we got cards of our own and could pick out what we
wanted to read. After a while we learned to use the
catalogue, to look up the books we want, or find out about
a subject for school. The librarians do their best to teach
us good library manners, which are to look after the books
and not to disturb people who are reading.

Some of the books I like best are by Eliza Orne White.
I said so to Daddy and he said, "I will take you to see her
some day. She is an old friend of your mother's and
mine." I was glad I was going to know a real author. We
went the next Sunday afternoon. The house was in the
woods at the foot of High Street Hill. It was on a little
hill of its own with a steep shady driveway. The house
was very dark but that does not matter to Miss White
because she is blind. She knows the way around her house
so well that she walks almost as if she could see, except
she puts her hand out to feel the doorways and the backs
of chairs.

The first thing I saw when I went into the house was
the portrait of Marcella, who was The Little Girl of Long
Ago. I like that book the best of all Miss White's books.
It is about her mother when she was a little girl, and the
portrait, she told us, was painted by Chester Harding,
who was her grandfather. Marcella has short hair, shorter

than mine, and she is wearing a fur cape. There are other portraits in the house and old, old furniture like my great grandmother's.

I brought my copy of When Molly Was Six and asked Miss White to write in it. She called to Miss Heywood, a friend of hers who helps her, to find her a pen and the friend dipped the pen in the ink and held Miss White's hand to show her the right place on the page. Then she wrote my name and hers and the friend said: "That's a very good signature."

Miss White showed us her typewriter. She writes her stories on it and then Miss Heywood reads what she has written to her and Miss White tells her if she wants any changes made and then Miss Heywood types it over again.

We had tea and Fairy gingerbread. There was a piano and another lady, I don't know who she was, came in and played on it. It was Chopin she played. Miss White liked it very much.

"I must listen while I can," she said to my father. "I am growing deaf and I suppose I cannot hear music much longer. You know I am used to being blind. Even when I was a little girl I could not see well. I've learned to see with my mind and my fingers. But being deaf seems more difficult."

"Did she grow deaf?" Susie asked.

"Yes," her grandmother said, "but she never lost her courage. She kept on writing almost to the end of her long life and making children see the things she could see only in her mind. Her house has gone now. Part of the new Veteran's Housing Project is where it used to stand.

I've often wondered where all the old chairs and clocks and portraits went. Then last year I was on Martha's Vineyard and my friends took me to see some friends of theirs. As soon as I went in the room I felt at home because the first thing I saw was The Little Girl of Long Ago with her short hair and her soft fur cape. Miss White had given the portrait to the owner of the house."

"*The Little Girl of Long Ago* is one of my favorite books too," Susie said. "Is there some more about it in the journal?"

"No, that's all. The next part is about Vermont."

"Oh good, please read it," said Susie, and her grandmother went on:

In the summer time when we go to Vermont we always take a box of library books along with us and it is exciting to be able to go and choose so many. In Vermont we stay at Kents' Corner. Daddy's mother lives next door to us. She has two houses on opposite sides of the road. She lives in whichever one she likes. We can always go into both houses because she never locks the door. Once a friend of hers from New York asked her to lock the door when they went to the chicken pie supper. Grandma did but she left the key in the lock. She said it would be easier to find when she came home than it would be if she put it under the mat. Grandma is pretty old-fashioned. She doesn't drive a car and she has never had an operation.

The house of hers I like best was built by Remember Kent in 1797. He came to Vermont with an ox team, following a blazed trail. The house is near the brook. You can hear the water all night running under the forget-menots. In whichever house Grandma lives there is always a white ironstone tureen full of the best doughnuts anywhere.

Grandma and Mother are making quilts this summer. Grandma knows how already. She sews beautifully. The quilt she is making has rosebuds on it and it is going to be mine, she says. Mother's pattern is called Rose of Le Moyne. The roses look more like tulips to me. Mother takes up something new about every year. Last year it was stenciled chairs. The year before it was photography. Sometimes she says she might write a book. I guess she will if she says so because when my mother makes plans, they happen.

Posy is my baby sister. She is much younger than Sam and me. She is beginning to talk a lot now. This house is getting too small for us since she came. Daddy and Mother have been looking for a bigger house where we can each have a bedroom and there will be a playroom for us.

Daddy always has something interesting in his briefcase when he comes home at night. Sometimes it is a new book or a magazine from France or England. Sometimes it is candy or coconut cakes from Bailey's or a special kind of cheese or a letter with foreign stamps. Tonight it was the deeds for our new house on Hawthorn Road. It is across the railroad near Muddy River and Jamaica Pond, not far from where my mother and her mother were born.

I guess we'll miss this part of the town where we know almost everyone we meet and everyone knows us. That's what happens, I suppose, when you live a long time in one place and when other people near you do the same thing. It's been fun to live so close to the center of the village in Brookline and to know so many of the people who look after the way the town is run. But perhaps it won't really be strange to us on High Street Hill because our great-aunt and great-grandmother have lived there and we know their houses. My great-aunt's house is lighted with gas instead of electricity.

Now we shall walk to school a different way and climb on different walls. A different elm tree will brush its twigs against our windows. Instead of the little hill on Thayer Street we'll go up and down the big hill on High Street when we go down to the village to shop. I think we shall miss the park most of all and all our friends big and little along the streets around it. But we can come back often on our bicycles and see them . . .

"Is this the house they moved to, right here where we are now?" Andrew asked.

"Yes, the very same house where, in just seven and a half minutes, you are going to bed," said his grandmother.

Andrew started to put his tools away.

"I'm glad they came here," he said. "I like it."

The next evening Andrew was making a model air-plane and Susie was using her new paints to make a picture for her mother. She had seen some Japanese paintings of fish under water and she was trying to make one herself. She kept crumpling the results and throwing them on the floor. "What is next in the trunk?" she asked as she threw about seven pictures into the fire.

Her grandmother picked up a book bound in soft blue leather. It had My Diary written on it in faded gold letters.

"Whose is that, Grandma?" Andrew asked.

"Well," said his grandmother, "I'll read you what it says on the front page: Louise Andrews, Heath Hill Avenue, Corner of Boylston Street and Chestnut Hill Avenue, Brookline, Massachusetts, United States of America, Western Hemisphere, The World, Solar System, The Universe. Private. Keep out. This means you!"

Susie laughed and asked, "Do you think you ought to read it to us?"

"I think I have the permission of the copyright owner," her grandmother said. "I'll read you a few things I've marked so you can see what it was like to live in Brookline in 1895 and a year or two after.

"January 7. Today was stormy. Mr. Lacy came and drove Oliver and me to school. We walked home. Got quite a few pungs the last mile."

"The last mile!" said Andrew. "How far was it and what are pungs?"

"We went to the Lawrence School in Longwood two and a half miles away," his grandmother said. "We alway$ walked except in bad weather.

A pung, she added, was a delivery wagon on runners. If the driver was friendly he would slow down and let you ride on the runners. S. S. Pierce's wagon was the best. It had two big dappled gray horses and it was so big that sometimes half a dozen children would be hanging on it. The driver was very jolly. Sometimes a pung would have a cross driver who would lash behind with his whip to keep you off. Sometimes, if you had got on without the driver noticing, some mean character on the sidewalk would yell out, "Cut, cut behind!" and the driver would lash back. The whip would sting right through your black cotton stockings and you would have to jump off into a snowdrift.

"Wasn't that dangerous if a car came along?" Susie asked.

"No, because there weren't any."

"No automobiles?"

"Not in Brookline," her grandmother said. "I'd heard

of a horseless carriage but I didn't believe in it."

"Did you have a telephone?"

"Yes. There weren't very many but we had one. We cranked a handle to ring Central — that's what we called the operator. She knew us and was very nice about getting the number for us. My grandmother had a telephone too although she was very old-fashioned. Grandmothers often are. She wore black silk dresses of such heavy silk that the wide skirts could almost stand up by themselves. The tops of the dresses were called basques. They fitted tightly and had little coattails behind. Her hair was parted in the middle and had curls that hung down at the side. They were very white. It was fun to see her make them by brushing them over a curling stick. In the house she wore a lace cap and outdoors a bonnet and a mantle trimmed with velvet and some black shiny stuff called jet. She never quite got used to the telephone and always stood a good way off from it and talked loud into it. Her voice was usually gentle but she didn't approve of electricity being let loose in the house and she felt safer if she didn't stand too near that box . . . Shall I read you some more of the diary?"

"Yes, please," they said.

Jan. 10. We walked to school today. G. B. and W. B., the mean old skunks, were waiting for us at Sumner and Boylston. They put us down in the snow and washed our faces.

Jan. 11. G. and W. were waiting for us again. This time they took our sandwiches. Oliver tried to knock them down and they made his nose bleed. Coming home

on Walnut Street I ran into a tree and made *my* nose
bleed. This is a bad day.

Jan. 12. There is a new store where Mrs. Cilley's used
to be. It is called Paine's. They have newspapers and
writing paper and lots of things for dolls' houses. I
bought some food for my dolls. A salmon on a white
ironstone platter and a dish of green peas and a dish of
wine jelly with whipped cream for dessert. They cost five
cents apiece. The dolls are pretty lucky. We had rice
pudding today. Ugh! Grandma says William Paine is
a very fine young man. He certainly is only of course he
isn't very young. He must be at least twenty-two. Oliver
spent his allowance, the whole ten cents, at Young and
Brown's on candy. He got bulls'-eyes, choc. cigarettes,
lemon drops, peppermint sticks, black jacks, liquorice,
and three choc. creams. He didn't eat much supper. It
was halibut with the kind of yellow sauce they make in
Holland. I scraped mine off. Papa says that someone
tried to get Young and Brown's number on the telephone
late last night and that he got Dr. Francis by mistake.
The man said, "Are you Young and Brown?" and the
doctor said, "No, I am old and gray." I laughed but
Oliver did not feel like laughing.

Jan. 19. Dr. Sabine came to see Oliver this morning.
He has a new fur cap and a coat with fur inside and lots
of braid outside. He says he thinks Oliver will recover.
I have a new coat. It is blue with brass buttons and the
sleeves are puffed at the top like Mamma's. It is just what
I wanted. Oliver's new sailor suit came home from
Jordan's. It had a silver whistle with it and a new fifty-

cent piece in the pocket. He says he is not going to buy any more candy but will start saving for a race horse. I have a new plaid dress for school. I don't like plaid but Mamma does.

Feb. 14. Katharine and I were waiting for the postman to see if we had any valentines and Bouncer chased us up on the fence and kept us there all the morning. Every time we tried to get down he would jump up and snap at our feet. Once he got mine and almost bit through my boot. It was my new lace-up black boot. I cried and K. said don't be a baby but pretty soon she was crying too. Boston terriers are supposed to be gentle but I guess Bouncer is part lion. At last the postman came and he saw us and chased Bouncer off with a stick and gave him a beating. I got eight valentines. Most of them had lace paper on them. Three were from Mamma. She disguised her handwriting but I knew it.

Feb. 21. They were ploughing out the streets today and I was running around the corner of Warren Street and I almost ran head into a big old brown shaggy horse. He was dragging a sidewalk plough which is a new improvement the town has. The men who were leaning on their shovels or sitting on the wall all laughed. It rained a little in the evening and then froze. There ought to be good coasting tomorrow.

Feb. 22. The crust was fine for coasting in the Atkinsons' pasture back of our house. We coasted almost to the Reservoir. Oliver says the Atkinsons' cows are bulls but I don't know if they are. Today we were coming up hill with our sleds and when we were almost at the top, one of the bulls bellowed and O. let his sled go and it slid all the way down. He said the bulls would come and trample it so I went down and got it. The bull kept bellowing and I thought I heard it coming uphill behind me. I didn't dare look back. When I got to the top, I looked and the only animal in sight was that old snow-plough horse, ploughing our sidewalk.

Feb. 23. This was the night of the sleigh ride. I wore my new coat and my black velvet hat with the ostrich feathers. I carried the chinchilla muff Papa gave me for Christmas and I had on my gloves that are lined with red silk so my hands were warm. Nothing was cold except the tip of my nose. We had a big pung with straw in it and lots of rugs — bearskin and wolfskin and green cloth lined with fur. Mamma wore her purple cape with the Van Dyke lace and velvet collar and the squirrel lining. We had two big black horses with silver bells on their collars. The bells rang all the way. The faster you go, the louder they ring. We sang Jingle Bells and There'll be a Hot Time in the Old Town Tonight and Fair Harvard and Tarara-Boom-de-Ay. One of Katharine's friends is in Harvard. He sang a song about a man who asked for bread with one fish ball and the waiter roared it through the hall, "We don't give bread with one fish ball!" I wouldn't care. I don't like fishballs anyway. One of Papa's English cousins tried one and he said "Waiter, something has died in this bun." Anyway we did not have any after the sleigh ride. We had hot chocolate with whipped cream and chicken sandwiches. Yum!

March 12. Boylston Street isn't muddy any longer when

we walk to school. Today the wind was blowing hard so the air was full of big clouds of dust. They sailed away above the elms. We came home by Walnut Street. It is longer but we dodge G.B. that way.

March 13. The gypsies have come. They are in their camp near Hammond's Pond. Bouncer went with us to look at the camp and got into a fight with a gypsy dog. He was a black dog with brown spots. Bouncer won. He always wins.

Everything about the gypsies seems either black or brown. The men and women and children all have black hair and eyes and brown faces. The tents and the horses and the dogs all seem to be brown or black. Of course their fires and the smoke aren't black but the kettles they cook in are black and their dishes are brown. Their stew smelled awfully good. Papa said, "No doubt it was. It probably had partridges out of your grandfather's woods in it."

March 19. Bouncer hasn't been home for three days now. I wore my yellow silk smock that Mamma brought me from Liberty's in England to dancing school today. I carried my best slippers in my new purple velvet bag. Oliver has a black suit with a button-up jacket and a stiff collar with a bright red tie. It was a nice day so we walked to Reservoir Station and went on the train. They have electric lights in the hall now. When they first come on, before they get warmed up, they are a soft pink for a minute and then they turn as bright as the sun almost.

We danced the waltz, the polka, the schottische, which is very hard, the Barn Dance, the Highland Fling, and the

Lancers. I was in a Lancers set with G.B. He doesn't
know his left foot from his right.

E.M. has pale green button boots that match her
dress. B.H. has bronze slippers. I am going to wish for
some on the Wishing Stone on the way home from school
tomorrow.

March 24. Bouncer hasn't come home yet. The gypsies
have gone away now.

April 1st. Oliver called up the Aquarium and asked if
Mr. Fish was there. The man banged the receiver pretty
hard.

April 5. It is very dusty and the watering carts are out.
The one that goes by our house has a white horse. O. and
I ran after it and got just as close as we could without
getting wet and dared each other to put our hands in the
sprinkler. Pretty soon we got splashing each other and
all of a sudden the driver turned the water on hard and
we were soaked.

Mamma saw us and sent us to bed. Sometimes I wish
she would just spank us instead of being modern. E.M.'s
mother has modern ideas too only she is allowed to save
up her punishments. Once she had two whole weeks of
bed ahead of her. Luckily she had the measles and her
mother let her count it as time in bed. She wasn't very
sick and they let her have lemonade and sponge cake.
She has curly hair too.

I read some of Vanity Fair in bed. I began in the upper
left-hand corner of the bookcase in the parlor and I am
going right through. I liked the Rose and the Ring better
than Vanity Fair. Mrs. Crawley is very mean to her little

boy in it. His name is Rawdon. Thackeray is my favorite
author.

April 4. We stopped at Grandma's on the way home
from school. She doesn't have any more mince turnovers
in the pantry now it is spring. We ate hard molasses
gingerbread and spiced white gingerbread and hermits.

April 25. Mamma has gone to Philadelphia and I am
staying at Grandma's on Irving Street. I have the Tower
Room for mine. It has eight sides and three windows.
The furniture has carved bunches of grapes on it. The
next room has a lot of books in it and a milking stool with
daisies painted on it. I guess my aunt painted it. She is
quite an artist. She and Mamma both embroider beautifully. They are making all kinds of things for a fair, which
is going to be for the benefit of the Woman's Exchange,
such as picture frames and book covers and sofa pillows.
I am making some needle books. Mamma embroiders
the cover and I am doing the rest.

April 26. Climbed the cherry tree today. A branch
broke and I fell out and tore my dress. Aunty mended it.
She said I was a visitor so I would not need to go to bed
only please keep out of the tree. That was pretty nice, I
think. I worked on my needle books all the evening. It is
rather quiet here. Grandma sits at the big table in the
library and writes letters and reads her big Bible. She
has a double German student lamp to read by. It gives
better light than the gas. The oil goes guggle-guggle in
it every now and then. The table has six drawers in it
and there are lots of interesting things in the drawers like
old daguerreotypes and big glass marbles and puzzles and

bottles of pills. They are homeopathic pills. They taste very good. I ate a whole bottle this afternoon.

April 26. At school today I asked the teacher if there was any special reason why some people subtracted from the right-hand side of the paper instead of from the left the way I do. She just looked at me and shook her head for about five minutes and then she said she was afraid I was not a natural mathematician and how did I ever get in the sixth grade? I said I skipped and she said she could well believe it. Then she made me rule a sheet of gray paper into four columns and then rule twenty-four lines across. That makes a hundred spaces, she says. She gave me an example in subtraction to put in each one. I wish I had not talked so much.

April 27. Mamma has come home. She bought me an amethyst heart on a gold chain. She has a new hat. It is made of two white roses and a green bird of paradise plume.

May 1. Last night our house caught fire. The cook went to bed with a lighted candle right beside her — for company, she said — and somehow the blanket got into the flame and caught fire. She didn't try to get it out but just screamed FIRE! FIRE! The rest of the family all carried pitchers of water and threw it on the fire and Papa told me to telephone the fire department so I did and very soon I heard the bells that tell where the fire is and the horses galloping up the street. The avenue was full of engines and horses and men in helmets. I unlocked the door and the men came in carrying big copper fire extinguishers. Some stayed outside and fastened the big hose to the hydrant. They didn't have to use any water. They got the fire out with just the extinguishers. It was almost out anyway but the room is a mess. Katy got over screaming and made coffee for the firemen and Mary served it. Papa gave them cigars. Oliver and I knew a lot of the firemen and the horses because we go to the fire

house on Saturdays and hang around in case there is a fire. Once in a while there is one and it is fun to see the horses stand in their places and the harness come down on top of them and the men slide down the poles and buckle all the straps of the harness so quickly. It's wonderful how soon they get going. The horses stand very still while they are being harnessed, just shaking their manes and pawing

the ground a little and then they gallop like anything.
When they get to the fire they stand still too. Once one
of our favorite horses, a beautiful big bay, slipped on
some ice while he was galloping and broke his leg and
they had to shoot him. G.B. laughed at Oliver and me
because we cried but Papa said it wasn't silly — that we
had lost a good friend.

May 2. Orioles are singing. I saw a scarlet tanager in a
big elm near Miss Amy Lowell's house.

Saturday. Bushway's cart came around today. Oliver
and I each bought a five-cent package of ice cream. He
got chocolate and I got strawberry and we took turns eating out of both packages. We have almost fifty Bushway
spoons saved up in case we go into business.

Sunday. We walked to church today. Then walked to
Grandma's for dinner. We had cream of tomato soup,
roast beef and Yorkshire pudding, mashed potato and
asparagus. The ice cream was coffee. I don't know why
anyone chooses coffee. I read Trilby after dinner. Du-
Maurier is my favorite author now. We walked home
afterwards and then Papa asked if we wouldn't like to
take a nice brisk walk before supper. I wish I had a bicycle. Supper was scalloped oysters. Apple blossoms are
out.

May 15 (I guess). Oliver and I had a lemonade stand
today. We had it at the foot of the avenue. We sold 9
glasses besides what we drank ourselves and made 45
cents. We saw lots of carriages and made a list of all the
kinds. Lots of ladies were out calling today and we saw
a barouche, two Victorias, a landau, a carryall, and a

coupé, besides hacks and carts. Mrs. Jack Gardner's carriage went by. It is a brougham. We knew it was coming a long way off because we heard the silver bell. Hers is the only carriage that has a silver bell in spring. We hear it first about the same time as the peepers start ringing in the swamps so then we know she has moved out to Brookline.

Miss Amy Lowell went past in her dog cart. Katy says that one of the maids at the Lowells' told her that once Miss Lowell saw a buggy being run away with and two little old ladies in it and didn't the horse run the buggy right into the ditch? And didn't Miss Lowell, she says, tie her own horse to a tree and lift that buggy right back on the road? It's that strong she is and goodhearted. Katy says she hurt her back doing it and lately she stays at home a good deal and writes poetry. She does not look like any of the poets in the big steel engraving Grandma has of American authors. Mostly they are men with whiskers. The ladies have hoop skirts and wreaths of flowers in their hair. Miss Lowell looks more sensible. If she ever gets her poems printed I will read them.

May 17. This is Papa's birthday. I gave him the patchwork cover for his little pillow that I made when I was doing my sewing stint every day last summer. It is made of pieces of my dresses. I can sew pretty well now. I can do over and over and featherstitching, hemming and gathering and tucking but I can't make good buttonholes yet. The scissors grinder came today. When Katy heard the bell, she ran out with three knives for him to sharpen. I hope it won't rain tomorrow. Mamma twists up my

hair at night in squares of white silk to make it curl.
When it rains the curl all comes out. I liked it better
when it was cut short like O.'s. They say I must look like
a lady. If you aren't one I don't see any sense in looking
like one.

May 20. I got sent to bed again this afternoon. So did
O. We don't know what for. Mamma forgot to say. It
might have been for eating all the chocolate cakes or perhaps for smoking grapevine or for calling G. B. a few
names Oliver learned lately. Anyway I watched a lovely
funeral going by while I was in bed. There were 43
hacks. They made a wonderful noise pounding and rum-
bling past. The people in the carriages just behind the
hearse always feel very sad and have the curtains pulled
down but I guess the ones farther back go for the ride
mostly. Later I saw a big dray loaded with barrels. It had
four gray horses. It made lots of noise. Express wagons
make plenty of noise too because of course they don't
have rubber tires like a carriage. I saw two of the most
beautiful girls ride past on bicycles. The blond one had
on a green velvet suit with tight knickerbockers and the
dark one was in bright red velvet. I stopped at the Wishing Stone yesterday and wished for a bicycle but if I get it
I will have to wear a divided skirt like Mamma's and K.'s.

May 25. This is my birthday. When I came down to
breakfast, the table was all trimmed with apple blossoms
and my plate had a wreath of pansies around it. Standing
right next to my chair and all dressed up with tulips and
apple blossoms was a BICYCLE. The handlebars shone like
silver and it has a bell. The saddle is brown leather and it

can move up and down. Oliver and I are both going to
learn on it so he'll be ready in case he gets one for his
birthday. Papa gave me a lesson before he went to town.
I rode almost to the peony bed before I fell off. I had
lots of books too and some paints from O. Katharine gave
me a lovely chandelier for the dolls' house. She bought it
at Paine's.

June 1. This was a very hot night and Papa took us
over to Beacon Street and we all went for a ride on the
electric cars. The open cars are on now. We were lucky
and got a seat right back of the motorman and there was
room for all five of us. The breeze rushed right across the
car and cooled us off. After a while we heard thunder
and then it began to rain. The conductor hurried along
the sides of the car, pulling down the striped curtains.
Some rain came in through the cracks and of course my
hair came uncurled but I didn't care. It was fun hearing
it hit the curtains and drum on the roof and swish under
the wheels.

June 5. When we were in the village today, Papa
showed me the door of the old Punch Bowl Tavern. He
says the Tavern was a very famous one, a big building
with lots of others added to it but it was taken down and
now this door is about all there is left of it. It is in a
house near the blacksmith's shop where he went to get
his horse shod.

June 15. We are packing up to go to Iron Bound.
First we are going on a train at night and will get to
Mount Desert Ferry in the morning. Then we go on a
steamboat to Bar Harbor and then Charlie will meet us

with the Black Boat and we'll row to the Island. Mamma says that this year Oliver can row in the bow and I can move one seat forward.

Oct. 15. Last night . . .

"Excuse me, Grandma," Susie said. "Aren't you going to tell about the Island?"

"It isn't exactly Brookline," her grandmother said.

"No, but it was their life, wasn't it? You said the book was going to be about how it was to be alive then. Isn't what you do in the summer just as important as a lot of old examples in subtraction?"

"It certainly was to me," her grandmother said. "Perhaps I'll tell something about it later. Right now I think you'll like this next item.

Oct. 15. Last night Oliver helped catch a burglar. He told us about it at breakfast and Papa thought it was just a dream. O. said the moon was shining in his eyes and he got up to pull the shade down. He heard a noise and looked down. A man was trying to get in the dining room window. He couldn't and he moved on to the next one. O. followed along upstairs while the man tried every window downstairs. At last he found a window unfastened. It was in Mamma's writing room. He got it open and was going to get in but Oliver tapped on the window and the man looked up and saw him and ran away.

Mamma said we'd better look for footprints because it had been raining and the ground would be soft. "You must have been reading Sherlock Holmes," Papa said, but he went and looked and sure enough there were prints

in the flower bed under the parlor window and the writ-
ing-room window was still open. So he telephoned the
police and in half an hour they came and they caught the
man and he had Mr. B.'s silver that he had stolen. Oliver
was a real hero. We had ice cream from Vogel's — maca-
roon and orange sherbert, O.'s favorites — to celebrate.

Oct. 21. Dinner today was boiled mutton with caper
sauce and rice pudding for dessert. I said what I thought
and was sent to bed.

Oct. Halloween. We went to M.'s and bobbed for
apples. I did not get any but I got a ring out of a pan of
flour with my teeth. It looks like a ruby.

Nov. 2. Papa heard me picking out the Blue Bells of
Scotland on the piano with one finger. He said, "Mary,
I can't stand this — get the child a teacher." So now I am
having piano lessons twice a week.

Nov. 4. Oliver and I both ride our bicycles to school
now so G.B. doesn't bother us. We whizz right past him
as he waddles along.

Jan. 11, 1896. Big snow drifts. G.B. puts us into them,
of course.

Jan. 15. We have a new light across the street. It is
called an arc light. It's very bright and makes a fizzing,
clicking noise. The lamp lighter still comes every night
to light the gas lights on our side of the street. O. and
I like to watch for him. He walks very fast and whistles
so we hear him coming while he is still in the shadows.
He is a little brown man. He carries a stick over his
shoulder. It is taller than he is. He reaches up and turns
something and the flame comes on. It is like a butterfly's

wing, blue and violet in the middle and gold on the edge
and it flutters like a butterfly too.

Jan. 20. I have a cold today and I have to stay in. The
hand organ man came. He has a brown face and very
white teeth and a black curly mustache. The organ is
very beautiful. It is painted bright green and gold. In
front is a picture of a lady dancing on one toe. She has
a pink dress and a red rose in her hair. The monkey sits
on the man's shoulder. He has a scarlet and gold coat and
cap. I don't know if he likes the music. He looks very
sad. The man played Santa Lucia and My Old Kentucky
Home. Then he took off his hat and bowed and smiled.
I sent Katy out with my shiniest ten-cent piece and she
put it in the monkey's tin cup. I like hand organs better
than hurdy gurdies and better than German bands. On
Christmas morning a German band always comes and
plays Silent Night very loud while it is still dark and papa
sends out some money right off.

Feb. 12. It snowed today so when we went to dancing
school, Mr. Lacy drove us. I wore my embroidered mull
from India and my pink and green Roman sash from
Italy. G.B. asked me to dance. "No thank you," I said.
"It's snowing outside and there might be *drifts.*" Afterwards we went into Pierce's downstairs. It smelled lovely,
of coffee and cigars and eau de cologne and cinnamon.
Papa met us and bought us a box of candy. It was pretty
cold going home in the horse cars but there was plenty
of straw in the bottom so our feet were warm. Oliver
said the seat cushions look like caterpillars and I guess
they do. They are orange and black and fuzzy. The

driver looks shaggy in his big bear-skin coat. Clouds of steam came out of the horses' mouths. Mr. Lacy met us at the village and drove us the rest of the way home. I went to sleep listening to the sleigh bells and when they stopped I woke up and we were at our own door.

March 15. The gypsies have come. One of the women wanted to tell my fortune. She grabbed my hand and wanted me to cross her palm with silver. I didn't.

March 16. I can play the Blue Bells of Scotland and the Happy Farmer pretty well with both hands now. My teacher is a Fraülein. That is German for Miss. Sometimes papa groans when I am practising but not so much as he used to before I had lessons. He plays beautifully himself. Every morning before breakfast he plays Gilbert and Sullivan.

March 18. The gypsies have gone.

March 20. The streets are deep in mud except where they are paved with bricks or cobblestones. The hacks that go to the funerals have to be careful not to get into mudholes and get stuck.

April 10. We are having Art in school now. Miss N. sliced a cucumber and told us to make a design for a wall-paper using the pattern of the seeds. I never knew that cucumbers were art. I thought art was like Mr. John S. Sargent's pictures. He comes to visit our friends the B.'s in the summer at the island. He usually paints a picture of Grandpa's wharf with the barnacles on it. I never saw any cucumbers in his pictures but I suppose they ought to be just as good as barnacles. If I were going to paint a picture I think I would like to do one the way it would look from the Nautilus in Twenty Thousand Leagues Under the Sea by Jules Verne. He is my favorite author.

April 24. This was the last day of dancing school. G.B. had a Little Lord Fauntleroy suit on. It was too tight for him and the red sash would hardly go around him. I never saw anyone look sillier. I felt sort of sorry for him because I guess it was handed down to him and his mother made him wear it. I danced with G. when he asked me and we got through the Portland Fancy all right. He only stepped on my feet once when we were chassee-ing. (I'm not sure how to spell that.) Between dances he told me all about his stamp collection and when he bowed to me afterwards he turned the color of his sash and said, "I'm sorry about the snowdrifts." I said that's all right which was a lie.

June 17. All last night there were firecrackers being shot off over in Charlestown and I couldn't sleep much. That is the way it always is the night before the 17th because it's Battle of Bunker Hill Day. We couldn't set off our firecrackers until today. I had five packages of Chinese firecrackers wrapped in red and gold paper and a stick of punk to light them with. At night there were fireworks. O. and I went up in the attic where we can see all over Boston. We saw stars and rockets and golden rain falling.

Sunday. It was a lovely warm afternoon and we all five went on our bicycles to ride around Jamaica Pond. There were hundreds and hundreds of bicycles and so many bells ringing that it sounded like sleigh bells. Some men have special bicycle suits with knickerbockers and caps

to match but Papa just puts clips around the bottoms of
his trousers to keep them from catching in the pedals.
Mamma wore her gray divided skirt, a pink shirtwaist,
and her stiff straw hat. O. and I wore our sailor suits. K.
has a pretty red bicycle suit.

Oct. 4. Today I saw an AUTOMOBILE right in Brookline
Village. Smoke was coming out of it behind and it made
an awful noise. Three horses ran away on Washington
Street and two on Boylston. O. and I were in McMahon's
grocery store doing an errand for Grandma. It is right
where the two streets come together so we could see all
the runaways. The one on Boylston almost came into the
store. He dragged the buggy right up on the sidewalk.
Then the automobile stopped and the driver had to get
out. He tried to make it go by twisting something in
front and then running back and twiddling something
inside. He did it about six times and all the boys around
yelled, "Get a horse! Get a horse!" At last it made an
awful bang and there was some more smoke and it began
going Pup-put-put and he jumped in quickly and drove
away towards Boston. I wished I could ride with him
but I don't suppose I shall ever know anyone who has a
car. I bet he was going ten miles an hour or even more.
He had a lady with him but she was all tied up in veils so
you couldn't see who she was. They both had on long
linen dusters. I guess he might get to Boston in half an
hour. I said so to one of the firemen. I know him because
he was there the night Katy's blanket got into the candle
and he said, "Well, maybe so, maybe so but I doubt if it
will ever be practical." The blacksmith was out watching

too and the firemen said to him, "We'll be needing horse shoes for a long time yet, Tim." Tim just gave a kind of a grumph and went back to his forge. Oliver and I went in and he let O. blow his bellows a while.

"I guess those were pretty ancient times, weren't they?" Andrew said.

Yes, they were — his grandmother told him — especially if you look back on them. Sometimes it seems as if the pictures people keep in their memories get to be like old prints where everyone is having a good time — dancing or skating or playing baseball or watching a horse race. If you judged by the prints you would think everyone always enjoyed life in beautiful clothes and that the weather was always sunny and the grass always green. Except of course when there was snow and that snow is always fresh and clean and has blue shadows in it. But not everyone was having a good time — not even in Brookline.

A few people lived in great luxury. A good many more lived comfortably. Their horses were beautifully groomed and their carriages were wonderfully polished. So were their boots. When they sat down to read at night it was by the light of lamps that had to be filled and cleaned and polished every day — but by some one else. Their clothes were washed and starched and ironed and put back in the right places in their bureaus and wardrobes. Everyday they ate delicious food they hadn't cooked from shining glass and china and silver they hadn't washed.

"Pretty soft," Andrew said.

Yes, his grandmother went on, for a few people. Most

people were not nearly so comfortable as they are now. They didn't have electricity. Anyone who lived through the hurricane of 1954 has some idea of what that means. It doesn't take many days of candle and lamp light, of no refrigerator and no oil burner and no washing machine to make you thankful that you didn't live in the gay nineties.

"They weren't gay for everyone by any means," she added. "I can remember when — in the richest town in the world — there were boys with ragged clothes and bare toes coming out through their shoes on raw winter days. I'd see them out trying to find something for their mothers to burn in their stoves. They had old wooden boxes mounted on rusty, rickety wheels. In the boxes they would collect twigs, broken branches, scraps of kindling dropped when a load was delivered at some big house. If they were lucky, they might find a lump of coal to take home. Unless, of course, the dogs chased them off."

They would go to the dump — she went on — between Brookline and Boston where the swamp was being made into land, and hunt over it for things they wanted. Perhaps they'd find some more old wheels or a cracked cup or a bent spoon. Sometimes there would be some coal that was only partly burned. I remember seeing a boy taking home a broken baseball bat and a doll without any hair. It was near Christmas time. He had an old umbrella too.

These children didn't have proper food. You could tell by their teeth. It's a long time since I saw a child in

Brookline who didn't have good clothes or good teeth. Probably the ragged boys I remember had a better time than the few Brookline boys who were dressed like Little Lord Fauntleroy in velvet suits and lace collars. The boys who hunted over the dumps had freedom, even if their toes were cold. Probably a boy who went out picking up firewood for his mother would never grow up into a completely useless or selfish man. All the advantages were not by any means the property of the comfortable people. Still, there's always a middle ground that's better than either extreme and I think Brookline boys look better now when they all wear blue jeans and clean plaid shirts than they did when some were dressed to show they were rich and others could not help showing by their clothes that they were poor.

The general health of people who live in Brookline is much better than it used to be. We have many more citizens and much less sickness. Diseases that were dreaded when I was a child — diphtheria, typhoid fever, tuberculosis — have become more and more rare. We didn't even know enough to be afraid of infantile paralysis. Being paralyzed, we were told when I was a little girl, was something that might happen to you if you slept in a freshly plastered room before the plaster had a chance to dry.

Doctors, some of whom have lived in Brookline, have been working patiently for years to find some way of protecting children against infantile paralysis. In 1954 tests of the Salk vaccine were made. At last, this very year, on the twelfth of April, 1955, we heard what seems to me the biggest piece of medical news that has been published in my lifetime — that the Salk vaccine is successful in protecting young children against infantile paralysis.

When we get farther back into Brookline's past, I'll tell you about how the very earliest experiments in protecting people against any disease were made here. Without the courage a Brookline doctor showed in making them, medical progress might have been delayed for many years.

Dr. Boylston, whose house I will show you, did his work more than two hundred years ago. Now our Brookline Health Department works so well that we take it for granted that we have clean eating places, clean pasteurized milk, and pure water for washing and drinking.

None of these things came to Brookline by accident. Neither did our clean streets, the public bath house where you went to swim, our library, or our parks and playgrounds. They have all meant years of work and planning.

Schools — she added as she folded up the papers and put them away — are something that always look fine about fifty years after the scholars are turned loose. Don't let anyone fool you about that. I'm sure modern schools are better in many ways than the old ones were. And don't — she said — pay any attention to anyone who tells you that school days are the happiest days of your life. Grandmothers have more fun than anyone.

1 8 6 5   The Station was Draped in Black   6

A<small>REN'T WE</small> ever going to get to the sword?" Andrew asked.

"Yes," his grandmother said, "we'll come to it soon. We'll move back again now to a time thirty years before I used to tramp through the snow to the Lawrence School and we'll be in Brookline at the time the Civil War came to an end. This sword had always meant to me that time when there were more young Brookline men in the Southern states than there were at home. Brookline had only seven hundred and thirty-eight men of voting age but more than seven hundred men from the town went to the war. That means, of course, that many of them went before they were old enough to vote. It also means that the thoughts of men too old to go, of boys too young, and of all women and girls were in the South. The names of Southern towns and rivers and mountains were as familiar as New England names, more familiar sometimes. People who had never left Brookline in their lives learned geography, Southern geography, in this tragic way.

The first time I ever saw the sword — she went on — I was doing what you were doing when you found it. I was crawling under the eaves of my grandmother's house, the house with the tower on Irving Street. I was living in the Tower Room. Next to it was a big room where my Uncle Jim's books and papers were kept and where there was space under the eaves suitable for crawling. I am afraid this sport was not approved of by my elders, because when I found the sword I never asked anyone about it. It was many years later that I noticed that it said C.S.N. on the hilt.

"What does that mean?" Susie asked.

"It stands for Confederate States Navy," her grandmother told her. "How it got under the eaves of a Brookline house is certainly mysterious. Perhaps a story my Uncle Jim wrote about a sword is true of this one. In his story David Pollard, a young officer in the Union Army, was sent to capture a group of Confederate blockade runners. During the struggle with the Confederates, David was wounded and captured by a Confederate officer who turned out to be David's Harvard roommate. It was a sad reunion for the young men, but Tom Randall did the best he could to care for David's wounds. By the time David was well again, Richmond had fallen. As the two men parted at the war's end, they exchanged swords. David's sword was hung up over the fireplace in the hall of the Randall plantation. Tom Randall's sword with C.S.N. on the hilt went north. When David Pollard went to California to seek his fortune, he left the sword with a young cousin to keep for him until he came back.

"It is still there, waiting for him, a memento of the most terrible of all wars, where brother fought against brother, friend against friend. Yet the exchange of swords in friendship is a sign that the wounds of that war will heal at last. I'll read you part of Jim's autobiography so you can see what it was like to live in Brookline at the time of the Civil War."

My name — he wrote — is James Barrett Edgerly. I am the oldest child of James Wheeler Edgerly and Sophronia Wilder Edgerly. I am writing this story of my life for my children and grandchildren. First I am going to tell you about my early years and then every year I will keep a diary and add any important events out of it to my autobiography.

I was born in Boston in 1852. In 1856 we moved to Brookline. We lived in a house on the Mill Dam. The Mill Dam is a straight street built right across the marshes between Brookline and Boston. My grandmother says that when she was a girl she had to go from Boston to Brookline by way of Roxbury because the Back Bay in between was all open water at high tide. First they built the Beacon Street part of the Mill Dam and then they built a piece to join it, which is the one where our house was. It was a very busy street with beautiful chaises and other kinds of carriages rolling in and out of Boston every day. Many market carts passed our old house too because market gardeners in Brookline grow fruit and vegetables for the Boston market.

When the tide is high it still comes in and covers up all the fens except for a few islands that stick up out of the water here and there. It looks very pretty then, especially on sunny days, but at low tide it is just a dirty marsh. People dumped things into it and we'd find rotten oranges and old boots along the shore. Sometimes boards would come ashore and we'd make rafts and go fishing. Lots of wild ducks lived in the marsh and I liked to watch them but heavy mists rose out of it at night and my father decided it was not a healthy place to live. He has a bad cough and my mother is always afraid it might turn into consumption.

"What's that?" asked Andrew.

"It was the old-fashioned name for tuberculosis," his grandmother said. "At that time no one knew that it was a contagious disease and there was no Health Department in Brookline that worked for the protection of people against diseases. Many people died of it every year. Nothing could be done to cure it because even the best doctors did not know what caused it."

"Did they move away from the marsh?" Susie asked.

"Yes," her grandmother said and went on reading:

In 1860 we moved to our new house on Harrison Place. It is a big house. My father had it built in the best and most modern style with a Mansard roof and big windows. His business is buying and selling houses and land and he understands about building so he knew just what the carpenters should do. We need a big house because we have a big family. There are my mother and father and six children — James, Lucinda, Martha, Mary, John, and Frederick. My Grandmother Barrett lives with us and then there are two hired girls and Michael, so there are twelve of us besides any visitors who come to stay. My mother chose very handsome modern rosewood furniture for the house and thick carpets that are like walking on a flower bed. There are also black walnut chairs with grapes carved on them and with velvet seats and there are heavy curtains to keep out the draft.

One strange thing about my father is that he likes old furniture made before the Revolution better than he does new things. He went off the other day to see about selling a house. When he came back in the chaise, driving Billy, another wagon came along behind and in it was something he calls a highboy. It has curved legs and brass handles, which he says are very beautiful. He also had a marble bust of Clytie in the chaise on the seat beside him and a Wedgwood copy of an old Roman vase, called the Portland vase. Clytie is a Greek, I guess. Father says my mother looks like her. They both have wavy hair but I think my mother looks much better than any old marble statue.

My sister Lucinda — we call her Lulu — and Martha are getting to be young ladies now. They spend most of their time embroidering things. They also make wax flowers and hair bracelets. They paint daisies on milking stools and bulrushes on screens. They draw pictures of bowls of fruit and marble hands in charcoal. My grand-mother offered to teach them to paint on velvet but that is not the style now so I guess they won't. She has a pic-ture she did on velvet. It has peaches and a big pineapple and grapes in a blue bowl. I like it but Lulu and Martha say it is old-fashioned.

Mary is a tomboy. She's my favorite. She's only six but she climbs trees better than most boys. I've taught her to catch a ball properly. She never squeals when she sees it coming the way most girls do. She isn't afraid of mice and snakes either. When I have fights with the boys from the Marsh, she helps me all she can.

I will say for Martha and Lu that they work for our soldiers. They sew shirts and knit mittens and stockings and make bandages. When we lost the Second Battle of Bull Run — and I bet we wouldn't have lost it if Dr. Ed Wild had been in command — the rebels captured great piles of our hospital stores. A telegram came one Satur-day night asking for more supplies. Mr. Ginery Twichell, who is president of the railroad, notified all the churches and got special trains ready. In every church women and girls made bandages and every family in town gave what-ever they could to help the wounded soldiers. They sent food and nightclothes and shirts and sheets and blankets. We men packed the boxes and carried them to the station. Mr. Twichell had two freight cars waiting there. By four o'clock Sunday they were filled. Boston and other towns filled eight more cars. There were a hundred tons of supplies. Mr. Twichell went with them to Washington on the train. Twenty-one surgeons and many volunteer nurses went along with him. At New York the supplies were unpacked and taken across the river in boats and then packed into other freight cars that were waiting on the Jersey side of the river. Before seven o'clock Tuesday morning those bandages that Lu and Martha and the others made were being used. The whole thing took only forty-eight hours.

My cousin, Bunny Lowe, and I are in the Cadet Corps — The Brookline Rifles. We didn't have any uniforms at first — just flat-topped caps like Army caps. We had to drill with wooden guns. Even our first Brookline soldiers didn't have proper guns either when they started drilling. They just used any old flintlocks left over from the Revolution that were hanging up over mantelpieces or up in attics. I guess some of them had been there ever since the Battle of Lexington. Now we have rifles and uniforms in the Rifle Corps and we sometimes are asked to other towns to give exhibition drills.

Our Brookline volunteers were in the very first regiment of Massachusetts troops. We are not a very big town — but more than seven hundred Brookline men have fought in the war. We are going to win it soon — that's what they say down at the post office. If we'd only had generals like Robert E. Lee and Stonewall Jackson, we'd have won long ago. That's what the men say at Coolidge's grocery store over at the corner. I believe it's true. Bunny said I talked like a copperhead when I told him that. He says Grant is better than any other general. The trouble is they didn't make him a general soon enough. I guess if they'd made Dr. Ed Wild a general earlier in the

war things would have been different. He's lost his left
arm now — he ordered it cut off himself when it was hit
— and his right hand was already crippled by a bullet,
but that didn't keep him out of the fighting.

Once, after they made him a general, his troops were
guarding some Army stores on the James River. A big
rebel force surrounded him and the commander sent him
a letter telling him he was surrounded and asking him to
surrender. Dr. Ed just wrote on the paper, "We will try it.
         Ed. A. Wild. Brig. Gen'l Vol's."
and sent it back. The rebels didn't get the stores.

Probably the war will be over before I get a chance to
go but anyway when we take Richmond, I bet Dr. Wild
will be there.

My brothers Johnny and Freddy are very small — four
and a half and three — so they'll never have a chance to
go to the war. They don't take much interest in it. John
has only just started to wear trousers. Fred is still in
dresses.

My father couldn't go to the war either on account of
his lungs. Four years ago the doctor said he had better
take a sea voyage for his health, so in the summer he sailed
on a schooner, a three-master, down to Maine. The
schooner carried all kinds of goods for the stores in the
little towns along the coast and traded them for lumber.
They went way up to Mt. Desert and all around Frenchman's Bay. When father got home, he looked much better, not nearly so thin as he did, and his cough was almost
gone. One of the first things he said to mother was: "I'm
afraid you won't like what I've bought," and she said,

"What is it — more plaster casts?"

She said that because the last time he went somewhere he came back with casts of the whole frieze that used to be on a Greek temple called the Parthenon.

He made us all guess what it was he'd bought this time. I asked if it was animal, vegetable, or mineral and he said it was all three but mostly mineral. After a while we got it out of him. He'd bought part of an island called Iron Bound Island and an old farmhouse and even some boats. There were wild sheep running around on the island, he said, and lobsters in the coves and bald eagles flying over it and caves with anemones growing in them. The cliffs were so high that a sixty-foot spruce at the top of one looked like a small bush. There was one tree with an osprey's nest in it that was big enough for Johnny to sleep in. He said the air was wonderful and he'd never felt so well and we'd go every summer. It was near Bar Harbor, he said.

I think Mother was a little disappointed at first because she loves the mountains — she had taken the girls to Elmore and Stowe in Vermont the summer before — but he told her that Iron Bound had sea and mountains too. As soon as she saw it, she loved it. We all do.

While their grandmother had been reading, Andrew and Susie had been looking at a pile of pictures of the Edgerly family. Some of the pictures were daguerreotypes. These are photographs on copper plates, which have to be shifted around in the light until you can see the picture. Others, she told them, were ambrotypes. These were glass plates with a dark background and they could see the pictures without turning the plate to catch the light. The small size was in its own gilt frame and said on the back that they cost twenty-five cents apiece. Their grandmother had labeled them on the back with names and dates so they could recognize the different members of the family. The man with the hollow cheeks and a shawl thrown over his shoulders was their great-great-grandfather, James Wheeler Edgerly. Men used to wear shawls at that time, their grandmother told them. Even President Lincoln wore a shawl sometimes instead of an overcoat. James Edgerly's wife had a wonderful bonnet with roses under the brim. Lucinda and Martha were very grown-up in their best plaid silk dresses. The children recognized Jimmy because of his soldier's cap. Freddy was wearing a low-necked short-sleeved dress. Mary looked very serious. The photographer had put a spot of pink on everybody's cheeks and red on their lips and a little yellow on Freddy's hair.

Susie said. "Please read some more of the diary, Grandma."

"All right — here's something about the big table that's upstairs in my writing room," her grandmother said.

March 21. The new table father had made to go with the highboy came home today. He designed it himself. It has six drawers in it and it is for us to sit at and study. Each of us has a drawer to keep books and papers in and whatever else we like. John put his book Slovenly Peter and his big glass marble in his drawer. Lu and Martha

filled theirs with notepaper and their albums and their
mother-of-pearl card cases. Mary put her stamp collection
in hers. She has quite a lot of stamps now, mostly U.S.
but a few foreign ones. I gave her one of my Cape of Good
Hope triangulars. Father gets lots of revenue stamps and
he gives them to us. My drawer got filled up soon because
I have so many school books and all my war maps. Freddy
wanted to put Edward Elephant in his drawer but Edward is too fat so Freddy played with him on the carpet
for a while, pulling the string that makes Edward say
"Toot, toot," and laughing. All of a sudden Fred went to
sleep right in the middle of the floor with his head on
Edward. Father picked him up and carried him up to
bed, elephant and all.

March 22. Freddy is sick today. He has a fever. When
I asked the doctor what it was, he said, "It is a febricular
fever." I know enough Latin to know that that means a
feverish fever. I told him so and he said: "Young man,
you are so sharp that you'll cut yourself if you don't look
out." If I were not going to be a soldier, I would like to
be a doctor — one who knew something. Perhaps I can
be both, like Dr. Wild.

March 23. Freddy still has his fever. Spring cleaning
is going on. I hate spring cleaning. All we had to eat for
dinner was cold beef and potatoes and beets and corn-
starch pudding. I would rather eat glue.

March 24. The doctor came twice today to see Freddy.
He still calls it febricular. There was a fire in the village
today and I ran along and helped pull the hose cart. I
carried father's fire bucket but we didn't have to use

buckets. We got the fire out just pumping from the well.

March 25. We got our ambrotypes today. Each one is in a frame that looks like gold. They are all good. We showed it to Freddy but he didn't notice it much. He didn't even smile. At the post office they are saying that our troops may march into Richmond soon but they have been saying that for a long time. Someone said he heard Dr. Wild, I mean General Wild, was with them and I bet he is. At the station the telegraph goes all the time. They say we'll hear the church bells ring when our troops take the city.

March 26. Freddy is a little better today. No news from Richmond.

March 27. The doctor was here twice last night.

April 2. Freddy died today.

April 3. We heard the bells ring today for the fall of Richmond.

Their grandmother stopped reading and Susie said: "That's very sad."

"Yes," her grandmother said, "and the saddest thing was that it wasn't unusual. Families were large in those days but there were many deaths of small children. There were eleven children born into the Edgerly family but only five of them grew up. The sixth drawer in the table was never needed."

I read you this part of the diary — she went on — because no picture of how people lived in the early years in Brookline is at all true unless it shows the difference in medical knowledge between then and now. In 1955 a child isn't sick with a febricular fever, which is just a way of saying that the doctor doesn't know what's the matter with him. Perhaps all he needs is a shot of penicillin and in a day or two he's as lively as ever. Whatever the trouble is, a Brookline doctor has all the resources of modern science at hand. Brookline children live near one of the great medical centers of the world and can be well cared for when they are ill. Better still, the town has health service to prevent illness before it starts.

Brookline was a pioneer town in the prevention of smallpox and by the time of the Civil War vaccination was widely practiced and it was unusual to see anyone whose face was scarred by this terrible disease.

"Did you ever see anyone who had had it?" Andrew asked.

"Yes," said his grandmother, "and I'm glad I'm not likely to now. When we get back to the time of the Revolution I'll tell you more about the part Brookline men played in the battle against smallpox, a battle just as important as any ever fought with guns. But now let's look at a copy of Jim's newspaper. Here it is."

"Why, it's printed!" Andrew said.

"And on his own printing press," his grandmother said. "This is volume one, number three of *The Brookline Banner,* April 15, 1866. Price five cents. James B. Edgerly Editor. Abram Lowe, Jr., Business Manager. This issue is dedicated to the memory of Abraham Lincoln on the first anniversary of his death. It begins with an account of Lincoln's life. I'll read you the last part of it.

"Governor Andrew had appointed the 19th of April, 1865 as a special day of celebration for the end of the war.

April 19th was the date of the first blow for freedom from
British tyranny, struck at Lexington and Concord in 1775.
It was also the anniversary of that day in 1861 when the
first Massachusetts troops were attacked by a mob as they
passed through Baltimore on their way to defend Washington. There was no celebration. All over the nation
it was a day of mourning. Our public buildings, even the
railway station, were draped in black. Abraham Lincoln,
the greatest American since George Washington, had died
by an assassin's bullet. He had died for a truly United
States, for freedom for all men as surely as did the men
who fought at Gettysburg. Some of us were too young to
fight with swords but we can still remember the words
of his Gettysburg address and fight in other ways to make
them come true."

After the Civil War — their grandmother went on —
Brookline began to grow rapidly. It had been a country
town where the chief business was farming. Food grown
here not only went a long way toward feeding Brookline
but helped feed Boston too and was even carried on some
of the many ships that left Boston for ports all over the
world.

Cattle, some of them raised on Brookline farms, some
of them from other places were often driven through the
village on their way to the slaughterhouse at Brighton.
This was still so thirty years later when I was a girl.

Where the railroad goes under Washington Street
there used to be a brook with a spreading shallow ford
where the cattle would stop and drink. When the railroad and the bridge above it were built, this ford was

done away with, so in 1871 the Brookline selectmen ordered a drinking trough set up for cattle and horses. It cost five hundred dollars.

"Wow! Pretty stylish cows!" Andrew commented.

"Stylish or not," his grandmother said, "they needed water and so did everyone else. Just after the Civil war came one of the most important changes in the town. Up to that time houses had their own private water supply. Some had wells and some had springs. In 1865 water pipes and sewers were being built and the selectmen ordered the first fire hydrants. It was even suggested that every house in the town should have water from the public system.

"For a while after the Civil War the Brookline firemen were still volunteers. Their two-wheeled hose cart, bought secondhand, was stored in a shed in the village. The volunteers pulled both this and a hook and ladder truck. Even after the first hydrants were working, leather buckets were still carried to fires in case there was no hydrant nearby, and lines were formed to the nearest well or stream."

The Brookline volunteers — she continued — felt some bitterness when the town finally decided in 1874 to have professional firemen. The volunteers had done a good job for the town and they felt that the professionals were not likely to do better. People who were in favor of a professional fire department felt — and said — that belonging to a fire company was mostly for the sake of excitement and to have an excuse for chowder parties, which were a favorite form of fire-company entertainment. Harsh things were said by both sides.

The sad truth was that, no matter how picturesque the painted buckets were or how much fun it was to beat another company to a fire, the town was rapidly outgrowing the system. Brookline was no longer a tree-shaded country village surrounded by farms and the beautiful summer estates of Boston merchants. Business blocks were being built along the village streets. The farms and summer estates were being cut up into building lots. New houses were springing up everywhere.

Up to the time of the Civil War a police force had never been needed in Brookline. There were constables who collected unpaid taxes and occasionally arrested someone who got into a fight at one of the Brookline taverns. Sometimes a cow or a horse wandered into a neighbor's garden and had to be driven off to the pound. However in 1869 a police force was organized. It consisted of one man. Later a one-man traffic squad was added to control reckless driving by hackmen.

Fortunately, from the point of view of the children, the races continued to go on for one man was not enough to stop them. Horses galloped. Carriages swayed and rumbled. Red-faced drivers in greenish black coats with silver buttons and tall hats cracked their whips. Passengers leaned out the windows and yelled encouragement, sometimes waving umbrellas. Dogs and small boys joined in the fun. It would have needed more than one traffic officer to moderate such activity.

Let's get this old copy of *The Brookline Chronicle* out of our trunk and look at the advertising — she suggested. Advertisements are always a good way to find out how people are living and this one will tell us a great deal about Brookline in 1874. Notice how much of the advertising is connected in some way with horses. Here's a buggy for sale, secondhand. Here's a copper weathervane of a horse that will look well on a stable. Carriages meet the trains at Longwood Station and will take passengers anywhere for fifteen cents and upwards according to the distance. You can rent a small house with a stable for $550 a year. A gentleman is going to Europe and would like to sell a fine double harness.

My father used to tell a story about a man who lived in Boston and who had a very beautiful trotting horse. Unfortunately the horse had a peculiarity. He would trot briskly out along the Mill Dam until he got to what is now St. Mary's Street. There he would stop short and no power on earth, not the whip lash nor shouts nor soft wheedlings nor lumps of sugar held in front of his nose would get him out of Boston and across the Brookline boundary. At last his owner decided to sell him and this is what he put in the paper: "Fine trotting horse for sale by gentleman who wishes to leave town."

Andrew laughed but Susie said conscientiously, "I don't think that was honest."

"And how right you are," her grandmother agreed. "The horse is a noble animal but there is probably no subject on which there has ever been any more dishonesty."

"Do you think people are more honest now?" Andrew asked.

"Yes, in some ways. There's a piece out of Jim Edgerly's diary that illustrates one of them. Here it is. They are at Iron Bound and it's jelly-making time."

August 2. Mary went with me to pick berries and we got 2 quarts of raspberries and four of wild cranberries. Mother started right away to make raspberry and cranberry jelly, which is my favorite. There is always a lot of sand in the sugar and when the jelly boils hard, scum comes to the top and the sand sort of sticks in it and Mother skims it off until there isn't any more. A little of it tastes good and we all came in the kitchen and shouted:

"Mother, we want the sand,
Mother, we want the grit,
Mother, we want the sand and grit!"
Until finally she said:
"Yes, you shall have the sand,
Yes, you shall have the grit
If you will eat it, every bit!"
So she gave us each a saucer of it and after the first spoonful, it was so sweet and sticky and sandy that we couldn't swallow it and I guess it will be a long time before we ask for that again.

"How did the sand get in there?" Andrew asked.

"The grocer put it in there to make it heavier," his grandmother told him.

"Packaging and proper labeling of goods," she went

on, "has made it almost automatic that you get what you pay for. Merchants found out that honesty was the best policy for sellers as well as for buyers. Most of our successful businesses are based on that fact."

Let's look at some more 1874 advertisements — she added. Here are some more things that you need if you have a horse — hay for him to eat, straw for his bedding, proper horse shoes from the blacksmith, a new sleigh or your old one re-painted, and buffalo robes to go in it. The horse has to be kept warm too while he's standing still. A fine blanket that will protect him from sickness costs $1.58.

Then there are all kinds of ornaments for lawns — vases, fountains, statues, cast iron deer, and stone lions. A lawn mower has been invented and has won a silver medal for its easy running. Here is a picture of a small boy pushing one. It is a nice warm summer day but he is wearing a coat, tie, waistcoat, knickerbockers, cap, and high boots. He is a remarkable boy. He looks cool and comfortable and not a button is out of place. When he gets through work, he can treat himself to either oriental or French confectionery at thirty cents a pound. Of course he probably can't afford it because he didn't get more than ten cents for mowing the lawn but he can buy five bull's-eyes for a penny. A bull's-eye is a hard candy a little smaller than a golf ball. Kept carefully in the cheek and sucked slowly, its peppermint flavor will last most of the afternoon.

There were all sorts of wonderful things listed for sale in the *Chronicle*. There were parlor organs and there was the Plimpton Parlor Bed, which looked rather like a parlor organ. It had pillars and a mirror and white marble shelves here and there. When it was folded up, no one who had not seen the advertisement would ever think it was a bed. The visitor would be much more likely to try to open it and sit down at it so he could play "Seeing Nellie Home." Like the organ it would take a lot of dusting and there was plenty of dust ready to fall on it. Coal and wood fires supplied a good amount and unpaved streets more. Some dust was carried into the house on boots in the form of mud and had to be dried before it could be removed with a feather duster. More blew in through the windows. Although there was a great deal of talk about a public water supply, it was not really working until 1874 so there were no watering carts to lay the dust.

However, the time was at hand. There is a special notice in this first number of the *Chronicle* saying that plumbing can be done for Charles River water pressure, and citizens of Brookline are notified that they can have water brought to their houses by coming to the Town Hall and signing a paper.

At about this time the Edgerlys moved away from Harrison Place to a new house on High Street Hill. Harrison Place was being cut right through their garden. It was to be called Kent Street. With the railroad running more and more trains every day on one side of them and delivery carts clattering along where their fruit trees and vines once grew, the house no longer seemed quiet and peaceful. Up on the hill an old farm was being cut into building lots and James Edgerly bought one of the lots and planted cherry trees and grapevines again. His wife planted iris and chrysanthemums, some of which still bloom every year.

The Edgerlys' new house and the others that soon grew up around it were ugly and solid and comfortable. They were so well built that they are still keeping people warm in winter and cool in summer. They had bathrooms and furnaces and wonderful built-in kitchen ranges that looked like pipe organs or folding parlor beds. They had ice chests too. These were a new invention. Usually things had been kept cool by putting them down cellar. An ice chest was a wonderful convenience. A big yellow ice cart came around several times a week. The cook put a card in the kitchen window showing how much ice she needed — twenty-five, fifty, seventy-five, or one hundred pounds. The iceman chipped off approximately the right amount, carried it in with his big tongs, leaving a trail of water and sawdust behind him, made a few seasonable jokes, chipped off enough ice so the door of the chest would shut, and left the cook to mop up. A cook was very lucky to live in a house with such modern improvements. She was paid four dollars a week besides.

The house was all lighted with gas, though there were still lamps to clean every day. No one used gas for cooking or heating. Electricity was still, in most people's minds, one of Benjamin Franklin's curious experiments. The furnace heated only the two lower floors of the Edgerly house. The boys slept in a big sunny room on the third floor and Mary had the tower room next door. The

cook had a fine warm room over the kitchen but the other
maids slept in another third-floor bedroom. These rooms
were so cold in winter that frost was thick on the windows.
Sometimes there was ice in the water pitchers. The children undressed downstairs in the bathroom, which was
deliciously hot, and then raced upstairs one by one and
jumped bravely into bed. They would keep their toes inside their flannel nightgowns — boys as well as girls wore
nightgowns — and gradually inch them out into the cold
bed. Sometimes by morning the bed would be almost
warm.

In summer the rooms were blazing hot under the slate
roofs, but that did not matter because in summer they
went to the island.

"How did they get there?" asked Andrew.

"First they were driven to a wharf in Boston Harbor.
There they got on board a schooner and sailed for several
days until they got to their own island. Then they and
all their belongings, including barrels of flour and sugar,
books and dogs and boxes of china, were landed on the
beach."

"You'll tell about it this time, won't you?" asked Susie.

"I'll tell you one story," her grandmother said, and
went on to tell them that James Edgerly made over a
small, pretty Maine farmhouse into another big ugly
comfortable house for his family. It was so big that there
was plenty of room for visitors, and a surprising number
of people crossed the four miles of Frenchman's Bay between Bar Harbor and the island.

One day a young Englishman hired an Indian to paddle him across the bay in a birch bark canoe. The bay was shining and calm and smooth as blue silk. They landed on a pebbly beach. The Indian did not speak much English but he seemed to understand that he was to wait. He lay down on the sunny side of a big spruce and began to smoke. His passenger had seen the big house from the water and he followed a grassy road up to it. There was no one on the long sunny porch facing the sea, but suddenly, he said, a girl, the most beautiful creature he had ever seen in his life, a girl with black wavy hair and enormous gray-green eyes, came running around the end of the house.

As he stood there watching her he said to himself: She's the one. Only she can't be more than twelve. Well, I'll just wait till she's old enough and ask her to marry me.

Out loud he asked if Mrs. Edgerly and Miss Lucinda were at home. They were and he was still there eating supper three hours later. At last he said he must go and that the lobster stew and the blueberry muffins were delicious and that he would like to come again, thank you.

Mary — that was the name of the girl he had decided to marry — and Johnny went down to the cove with him. They liked him. John especially liked his English clothes and his different way of speaking and his beautiful whiskers. John told him that he was ten years old and that Mary was twelve. The young man said goodbye and thanks for seeing me off. While he was saying this aloud, to himself he was saying: Six years. In six years — or perhaps five, I'll ask her.

John and Mary caught a few jellyfish and threw them

at each other and went back to the house. By the time they got there, the wind had changed and was coming in hard from the east. The tide was running out against it and there were white waves all over the bay. The family were all on the porch anxiously watching the canoe being tossed around like a chip in the white and green water. Suddenly the fog drifted in and hid it from their sight.

"I'm afraid," said Mrs. Edgerly, "that we shall never see that young man again."

"Did they?" asked Susie.

"We wouldn't be sitting here if they hadn't," said her grandmother. "You see he was my father."

"Did he wait the six years?"

"Yes he waited until Mary had graduated from the Brookline High School — she was sixteen then — and until she had studied two years more at a school in Boston so that she could take the Harvard Examinations."

"Was she going to college — to Harvard?"

"No. Girls were not considered intelligent enough to go to college but if they could pass the Harvard Examinations, it helped them to get a teaching position and Mary wanted to teach."

"Girls are dumb," said Andrew. "What did she study?"

"Perhaps this will give you an idea," his grandmother said. "One morning Miss Hubbard, the head of the school, found Mary playing cat's cradle by herself. It's harder than it looks."

"I'll say it is," said Susie.

"Mary," said Miss Hubbard, "have you prepared your English History lesson?"

"Yes, Miss Hubbard."

"And your Geometry?"

"Yes, Miss Hubbard."

She had also, it seemed, studied her French, German, Latin, Algebra, and American History. She had written a three-page composition.

"I think, Mary," said Miss Hubbard, "that you had better give me that string and I had better give you a new subject."

"So that, Andrew, is how your great-grandmother happened to learn Greek."

"How did she get to school in Boston? Did she walk?" asked Susie.

"Only part-way. She took the eight-fifteen train from Brookline Station. She set out every morning at the same time, carrying her green bag full of books. This was the same train that businessmen took to town. Farms and vegetable gardens had almost disappeared from Brookline. More and more men who worked in Boston lived in Brookline and took the train to town and back every day."

One beautiful May morning Mary turned the corner of High Street at her usual time. She stopped a minute to watch an oriole weaving his nest and then, not because she was late but because she felt like it, she began to run.

She ran all the way to the station. The last few yards she heard feet pounding behind her but she ran on. When she got to the platform, she turned. Running down the last slope to the station were lawyers with green bags, bankers with their flat-topped hats, rosy young businessmen with mutton chop whiskers, thin businessmen with white goatees, jolly young clerks with bushy black beards — or red or brown or even yellow. They came puffing down Station Street with the tails of their broadcloth coats flying. They stopped and looked for the train and wiped their faces, some with silk handkerchiefs of gorgeous colors and patterns, some with fine plain linen. When they got their breath again, they all began to laugh because they realized that they all had been setting their watches by Mary Edgerly.

Are you going to read some more to us?" asked Andrew the next evening.

"No," his grandmother said. "Tonight I'm going back another thirty years and I'm going to tell you about my friend Edward Atkinson and some of the things he remembered when he was a boy in Brookline."

Edward Atkinson — she went on — was a leading citizen of the town for many years. He was born in Brookline on the tenth of February, 1827, so in 1835, the first year he tells about, he was eight years old. He lived in a big house near the corner of Waverly and Cypress Streets.

Cypress Street, called the New Lane then, was so narrow that if an old one-horse chaise was jogging along ahead of you, your horse would have to jog along behind it all the way. There was no room to pass. The lane was thickly shaded by trees and bushes. Where the High

School is today, there were open fields bordered by stone walls. Part of the land was used for market gardens and part for pasturing horses.

Not far from Edward's house, on Washington Street, across from where the Public Library now stands, was a blacksmith's shop. Edward spent a good deal of time there straightening horseshoe nails that had been pulled out of old shoes while he listened to the sound of the smith's hammer on the anvil. He liked the big bellows that made the fire glow so fiercely, the changing color of the hot horseshoes — white, red, black — the smell of singeing hair and horn as the shoe was fitted to the horse's hoof. He enjoyed straightening the nails but he had an even more important task. This was to carry love letters from the smith to one of the girls who worked in the Atkinsons' kitchen.

On the morning he first tells about, however, he was not at the shop. Perhaps he was waiting to take an answer back to one of those letters. Anyway he was leaning on the fence looking down the New Lane. Edward's father, Amos Atkinson, was a Boston merchant. When he was at home he drove into the city every day in his chaise but it was a long time since the chaise had driven over the Mill Dam to town. One of his ships had gone to St. Petersburg in Russia and Mr. Atkinson had gone there to see about selling the cargo.

"He went to Russia?" said Andrew. "You mean to say we traded with Russia and just anyone could go there who felt like it?"

"Yes," his grandmother said. "The journey took much

longer then than it would now, but people from Boston went to Russia quite freely and did business there. It would seem strange to Amos Atkinson, no doubt, if he could know that with all our planes and fast ships we cannot just make up our minds to go to Russia or Hungary and then go."

"Was the journey very dangerous then?" Susie asked.

"Yes," her grandmother said. "Any sailing voyage was dangerous. Ships from Boston sailed all over the world. They were well-commanded and well-built ships and most of them came safely back to port but every now and then a ship would sail and never be heard of again. Or her owners would hear that she had been blown by a gale on some rocky coast and broken to pieces. Many of her crew would never come home."

Amos Atkinson — she went on — faced something more dangerous than shipwreck when he made his trip to St. Petersburg. There was an epidemic of cholera in St. Petersburg so bad that three people were not allowed to stand together in the streets. Nevertheless he made the long journey safely. He landed not at Boston but at Newport, Rhode Island, and then was driven across country to Brookline. He had been gone so long that his own son, Edward, leaning across the fence and seeing a carriage drive along the New Lane, wondered who the stranger was who got out of it.

"I expect he hurried right down to the blacksmith's shop and told the news," Andrew said. "Did he do anything else but pound nails there? Did he play any games?"

His grandmother said that where there were boys there

were always games. When Edward was a boy most families in Brookline kept a cow and a pig. In the autumn
the pig was killed and the pork packed away for winter
use. Some of it was salted, some made into sausage, some
smoked for hams and bacon. The pig's bladder would be
cleaned and given to the boys of the family. It would be
put into a leather case, perhaps of the pig's skin tanned,
and the boys would play football with it. They used to
play catch with a ball about the size of a baseball. They
made these balls, Edward writes, by cutting their old
gum boots into strips and winding them for the stuffing
of the ball. The outside they made of yarn and heavy
linen thread.

"What were gum boots?" Susie asked.

Her grandmother said they were heavy boots that came
from South America. They were made partly of rubber
and partly of clay. Women and girls had thinner and
lighter ones called India rubbers. Not all boys had gum
boots. Many wore cowhide boots — there were no rights
and lefts — which were carefully greased to keep them
flexible and waterproof.

These boys — and girls too — had plenty of fun. Edward tells how the boys used to walk over to Jamaica
Pond, undress among the trees and go swimming. Sometimes in summer eight or ten carryalls full of boys and
girls would drive over to Spot Pond in Cambridge for a
picnic. In winter both boys and girls skated on Ward's
Pond and lighted fires on the bank or coasted on Brookline hills. Wright's Hill, Heath Hill, Fisher Hill were
all favorite coasting places. Even Corey Hill, steepest

of all, was used for coasting and smaller slopes were alive with sleds on snowy days.

The children who were out coasting on the evening of January 21, 1837 — Edward may have been one of them — saw something they never forgot: the Great Aurora. This was a display of northern lights that made the sky such a brilliant red from east to west and from north to south that people thought the world was coming to an end in flames. In some places the volunteer fire companies were called out. In New York and Philadelphia the engines traveled for miles looking for the fire. Even the snow was red. White houses glowed crimson in the strange light and bare trees were like burning torches. It took so long for news to travel then that it was a week before people in Massachusetts learned how far south the Aurora had been seen.

Not only was there no telegraph in that year but the railroad had not yet come to Brookline. The Brighton stage came through the Punch Bowl Village, as it was called, once a week. The passengers were chiefly drovers who were going to buy cattle at Brighton Market. The men who were going to sell the cattle came on foot. They drove their animals into the stream that ran through the village and let them drink there.

The village took its name from the Punch Bowl Tavern. This old tavern, a Brookline landmark for more than a hundred years, was in its last days in Edward Atkinson's boyhood. He could just remember it when the drovers used to stop there for dinner and when their teams would be hitched all the way along Washington Street as far as

Harrison Place. The old sign was faded in Edward's time but it still hung there with its big punch bowl and ladle, a memento of the time when customers of shops and taverns could not read. The teamsters were sure of a good meal and a blazing fire on cold days at the Punch Bowl. There were no furnaces in those days. Open fires were the usual way of warming a room. That is, the fire warmed the part of the room near the fireplace. Fires in bedrooms were an uncommon luxury, but in the Atkinson house on extra-cold nights a polished brass warming pan full of hot coals was pushed in between the sheets and moved around until the icy chill of the bed had been changed to a delicious warmth.

"Alas," Edward Atkinson wrote many years later, "for modern children who will never know the luxury of a warming pan!"

Edward had many memories of the First Parish Church. In Brookline's early days this had been the only church in town but in Edward's boyhood there were two, for the Baptists had built their church where the road to Cambridge split off from Washington Street. Its steeple was already a landmark in the village. The First Parish Church was on Walnut Street. There were then, as there are now, plenty of rocks around it and the church was built right on the solid rock with no cellar. Like the tavern and houses and shops of the time, the church had no furnace, but it had two iron stoves with long pipes. Buckets hung at the ends of the pipes so that creosote ran down into them instead of running down on the floor and the seats. Wood fires were made in the stoves and the pipes

circulated some heat — and doubtless at times a good
deal of smoke — through the building. The ladies of
the congregation brought foot stoves filled with hot coals

with them and when their own feet were warm, passed
the stoves around hospitably. A foot stove tucked underneath the wide skirts and layers of petticoats that women
wore at this time must have produced a certain coziness
from the waist down. Above the waist were layers of
shawls, the outside one being often a Paisley shawl or
perhaps one of the beautiful cashmere shawls from India
of which Paisleys were an imitation. Enormous bonnets,
looking rather like the top of a chaise kept the ladies'
heads warm. They could doze through a long sermon in
the shadow of their bonnet and no one could be sure they
were not awake. People however did not sleep while Dr.
Pierce preached.

This remarkable man was pastor of the First Parish
Church for more than fifty years beginning in 1779. He
was so loved and respected in the town that a remark,

often quoted, was that "Dr. Piece is Brookline and Brookline is Dr. Pierce." When he first came to be the town's minister, there were six hundred and five inhabitants of the town. He learned to know them all — their names, their faces, their houses and gardens, the dates of their births and deaths. He never forgot a child he had baptized, either from the old pewter baptismal bowl he found when he first came to the church or from the handsome new silver one, given by the rich Mr. Hyslop and costing forty-seven dollars. Once, when Dr. Pierce could not tell the birthplace of a certain man, it was said that it was no use trying to find out because "if the Doctor did not know where the man was born, he was not born anywhere."

Dr. Pierce was a fine-looking, tall, wide-shouldered man, cheerful, kindly, and courteous. As a young man, his hair had begun to turn gray and it was a beautiful snowy white long before he was old. Until a short time before his death he had never had a day's illness. He used to get up early in the morning and either saw and split wood for the fires or work in his garden for two hours before breakfast.

Ministers sometimes preached in each other's churches and since the churches were few, it might mean a journey of six or seven miles. Some ministers used to drive the distance but Dr. Pierce used to go the whole way on foot, preach his sermon, and walk briskly back, timing himself by his big old-fashioned watch. He liked to tell when he came home how long the trip had taken.

For many years his salary was four hundred dollars.

The church also gave him the parsonage to live in and a supply of firewood every year. He kept careful accounts of everything he received. He set a value on the services of the ladies of the congregation who came in to help when his daughters were married. He noted the value of presents of pork and potatoes. All his accounts were kept in pounds, shillings, and pence.

Dr. Pierce loved music. Edward Atkinson remembered how the old minister used to sit with his hand to his ear waiting for the tune to be announced and join in the singing with his deep bass voice. The choir leader, who chose the tunes, was Mr. Ben Davis. There was no organ but the voices of the choir were accompanied by several instruments — clarinet, trumpet, bombardon, flute, and double bass.

In the church there were many interesting people whom Edward knew. There was Miss Prudy Heath, for instance. She was born in 1751 and to Brookline children in 1835 she was as much a part of the town as the Wishing Stone or the old fort on Muddy River near the Boston line, or the old stones in the graveyard. With her big green umbrella and her immense black straw bonnet, she was a familiar sight to Edward as she walked along the roadside, picking the leaves of blue chicory. She dried these and used them to make what she called "tea." She drank this tea except when she had company. Then she would bring out her best China tea and her quince marmalade — which she called "presarved squince" — and the finest cake she could make. To entertain Dr. Pierce and his family at tea was her greatest pleasure.

Out of a very small income Miss Prudy saved enough to contribute something toward the minister's living expenses. She also, while drinking chicory instead of China tea, saved enough to buy two silver cups for the church which are still among its treasures.

She lived to a great age, long enough so that she heard about the coming of the railroad. She was too old-fashioned ever to think of riding on a train but she did go over to Roxbury and look at the tracks. The picture she had in her mind of a train was a kind of especially mischievous and dangerous stagecoach. A stagecoach was strange enough to her eighteenth-century ideas but this new invention was so extraordinary that she could not even remember the name for it.

"Would you," she asked her friends over and over again, "would you ride in one of those ravin' stages?"

Another Brookline figure, known to children in both the eighteenth and nineteeth centuries, was Polly Hatch, who lived with Dr. Pierce's family for forty years. Her devoted service did a great deal to help the minister's salary meet the family's needs, so much that in many minds Polly was regarded as a kind of assistant minister. Polly herself would have been the first to contradict such a notion. She was one of a family of twelve children. They were poor and when their house burned down, Polly, only six years old, was taken in by the family of Dr. Pierce's wife. It was the custom in those days to have what were called "bound" girls and boys, children who worked without wages until they were of age. They were fed, clothed, and taught how to work. Polly Hatch learned how to make bread when she was so small that she had to stand on a stool to reach the breadboard and knead the dough.

When she was older she received wages but they were very small, as was the custom of the time. In a prosperous household the cook might be paid two dollars a week. The Pierces could not, of course, afford any such sum. Polly spent almost nothing on clothes but wore all her life what was given to her by members of the parish. Out of her savings she often bought for the Pierce children toys or books that they otherwise would have gone without. The children followed her wherever she went and she was never too busy to hear them read aloud. Scott's poems were her favorites and, from hearing the children read, she learned many lines of *Marmion* and of *The Lady of the Lake* by heart. She would repeat them to the younger children as she ironed their dresses. Polly did all the washing and ironing and cooking and cleaning and had time to take care of the children besides.

The Pierces had no cistern to hold rain water. All the water had to be carried from the well. Dr. Pierce had often said that he hoped to put in a cistern some day, as it would be a great convenience. While he was away on a journey, Polly hired a carpenter and paid him fifty dollars out of her own savings to build a cistern. When Dr. Pierce came home he was much pleased but said that he wanted to pay for the cistern himself. Polly burst into tears, saying she had had it done to surprise the family. It would break her heart, she said, if he said another word about it. Dr. Pierce let her have her way but he did not forget.

Everyone depended on Polly's good sense; not just the Pierces but other people in the parish and in the town. Whenever there was a problem to be solved, someone would be sure to say: "Ask Polly!"

On the twelfth of August, 1834, the church was struck by lightning. It happened that a town meeting was going on in the old stone Town House next to the church. It is still standing and is connected now with the present church building. It is called Pierce Hall in memory of Dr. Pierce. On the August day when flames and smoke appeared on the church roof, one of the selectmen of the town ran down to the parsonage shouting, "Polly! Polly! Polly!" Apparently he had no doubt that Polly could put out a fire on the meetinghouse roof. Perhaps she helped with advice, perhaps the water from her cistern came in handy. In any event the fire was quickly put out.

Another old lady whom Edward Atkinson knew was Miss Anna Dana. When he went to the blacksmith's, he used to drop in to see her in her house across the street. He would find her sitting by a woodfire, he wrote, with seedcakes under a glass cover on the table beside her. Edward must have been a favorite of hers because she regarded boys in general as her particular enemies and carried on a standing feud with them. She did not see where the children came from, she would say disapprovingly, and add that they were thicker than oak leaves.

If she saw two boys passing quietly by her house, she would go to the door and call out to them sharply that they must not shake her fence or throw stones at her house. These commands usually produced a good deal of fence shaking and stone throwing. It is perhaps no wonder that she preferred cats to boys. She sometimes, Edward remembered, had a dozen cats at one time.

He liked her house, an old-fashioned one, built around a huge central chimney stack. Great logs were burned in the fireplace of the east room. There were two brick ovens in the chimney. Perhaps the seedcakes were baked in one of them. The chimney was so big that Edward could look up it and see the sky. Sometimes, when the fire was out, snow drifted down over the logs. Miss Dana liked fresh air and for forty years kept an attic window open night and day. She felt that her great age — she lived to be over ninety — was due to this open window.

She remembered stories about Massachusetts in colonial days and would begin, "In my father's lifetime . . ." and follow with some tale of life under King George. She had watched the Battle of Bunker Hill from a housetop in Boston. Although her father had supplied Washington's army, she had Tory sympathies and a great admiration for the royal family. One of her great treasures was a big china bowl with the words, "Success to British Arms!" painted on it. During the Revolution, she told Edward, they had to keep it hidden.

When he was older, Edward wished that he had listened with more attention to her stories of old times instead of just thinking about when she was going to pass those seedcakes. Since he was often given this treat, he must have passed Miss Dana's test of good manners, which was never to put a finger on her big, highly polished round mahogany table. The floor it stood on was covered with

sand swirled with the broom into patterns. Across the
room from the shining table was an old desk piled high
with books. Above it was a dim, old long mirror. There
were two ancient chairs covered with old needlework.
The chairs, Miss Dana said, had once belonged to Governor Hutchinson of Massachusetts.

All the time Edward was growing up, there was much
talk in Brookline about slavery. Many people think that
all the inhabitants of New England were opposed to
slavery. It is true that Massachusetts was one of the early
states to declare slavery illegal, but it is also true that
New England sea captains carried on the slave trade for
many years. Boston and the towns around it were always
considered the center of the anti-slavery movement. Still,
it took a long time to educate the people to see the injustice of slavery and to see that it was especially unjust in
the United States, which had been established on the principle of liberty and justice for all men.

Mr. Samuel Philbrick, who lived in a big, square gray-
stone house on Walnut Street, was one of the first men
who had the courage to speak out for the abolition of
slavery. He was a Quaker by birth but he and his family
went on Sundays to the First Parish Church where he
owned one of the pews.

He was a friend of William Lloyd Garrison and of
Wendell Phillips and of other abolitionists. The gray
stone house — still standing in 1955 and not greatly
changed — was one of the stations in the Underground
Railroad. This was the system by which slaves who suc-
ceeded in escaping from the South were passed along

secretly from one family to another and sheltered until at last they reached Canada and freedom.

Although slavery was illegal in Massachusetts, the Supreme Court had decided that a fugitive slave, caught anywhere in the United States, could be returned to his master just as a horse or a dog that had wandered away might be returned. The first women who ever spoke publicly in Brookline against slavery were the Misses Grimké. They were daughters of Judge Grimké of South Carolina and they knew at first hand what slavery was like. They spent the winter of 1836–1837 in the Philbrick house and the first audience to whom they spoke met in Mr. Philbrick's parlors. The only man present was the Quaker poet John Greenleaf Whittier. Either because he was shy or because he thought the speakers might be shy in his presence, he hid himself in another room and was not seen by the audience. Some of his poems about liberty are said to have been inspired by what he heard that afternoon.

It was impossible at that time to hold an anti-slavery meeting in a public hall or even in a church. In Boston, when the Ladies' Anti-Slavery Society tried to hold a public meeting, a mob gathered and threatened to tar and feather the speaker. The meeting was broken up. The mayor of the city was present but instead of protecting the speaker, he simply told the ladies that they were arousing the mob and advised them to go home. There was only one minister in the city, Henry Ware, Jr., who had been brave enough to read the notice of the meeting.

After that, for a long time meetings were held in private houses and announced by cards of invitation to friends.

During the winter that the Grimké sisters stayed in the Philbrick house, great excitement occurred in Brookline over a very small Negro child. She was the daughter of a free colored woman who was struggling to support her children. To help her, Mrs. Philbrick took one of the little girls into her family. As would have been the case with a white child at the time, this small colored girl was to learn to make herself useful, at first for her food and clothes and shelter, later for wages.

The first Sunday after she came, she was taken to the First Parish Church and seated with the Philbrick family in their pew. She was so small that her head did not reach the top rail and she could not be seen during the service except by those in the nearest pews. However, she had been seen, coming in and going out. Aristocratic noses were turned up at such a sight. Before the next Sunday, everyone in Brookline had an opinion on the subject. Boys called the little girl names when they saw her on the street. The Philbrick children were teased about being "bobolitionists." However, the child was taken to church again. She hid behind the skirts of one of the older girls as well as she could, and again sat in the Philbrick pew.

One of the aristocratic upholders of slavery arrived after the Philbricks did. While standing up in his own pew, he could not see the little girl, so he sent one of his own children down the aisle to look into the pew and see if she was there. The child came back and reported that such was indeed the case. His father, with vast dignity, then gathered his family together and left the church.

This seems almost too ridiculous to be true, but there was not merely one family involved: many of the congregation were offended. Even Dr. Pierce, a kind and Christian man as well as a minister, agreed with a committee of the church members that if the Negro child came to worship God, she should do so from the gallery in a pew that had been set apart for Negroes when the church was built.

Mr. Philbrick refused to put himself in the position of saying one thing about the rights of Negroes and doing another. He also felt, since according to the custom of the church, he owned his pew as much as he did his house, he should have the right to say who should sit there. Since the committee disagreed with him, he decided that he did not care to worship in a church where such an un-Christian spirit had been aroused. He and his family left the First Parish Society and never entered the church again.

The station in the Underground Railroad continued its work for many years. It was a well-kept secret, but my grandmother remembered seeing a certain red flannel petticoat hung out on the Philbrick clothesline among the white petticoats and knew that it was the signal that some fugitive slave could safely enter the Philbrick house.

Famous in Brookline among these fugitives were William and Ellen Crafts. They were married and they dreaded being separated by the sale of one of them to another slaveowner. This happened to other Negro husbands and wives and they had reason to fear that it might happen to them.

Ellen was a tall, handsome, light-skinned woman, almost white. She disguised herself as a young Southern gentleman traveling for pleasure and William acted as the young master's colored servant. As the slave catchers were looking for a man and a woman, they were thrown off the trail by this scheme. Still, there were narrow escapes. Even in Brookline William and Ellen were in danger. They were first taken to a house on Cypress Street but it was decided that they were not safe there and that they must be moved. That afternoon the red petticoat was hung out on the Philbrick clothesline and after dark the fugitives were taken secretly to the stone house. For days they stayed in a dark little room at the back of the house while the United States Marshal and officers were hunting all over Boston for them. At last the Marshal gave up and turned to another place.

One night a carriage came to the Philbricks' door — the red petticoat signal was hanging on the line again. The young southern gentleman and his servant were started on their way to Canada.

"Do you suppose Edward Atkinson ever saw William and Ellen?" Andrew asked.

"He may have known about them. He was a great friend of Mr. Philbrick's son, Edward. They used to study mathematics and French and German together after they left school. They played chess together too."

"I'd like to know what Edward Atkinson did when he grew up," Andrew said.

His grandmother told him that in 1842, when Edward was fifteen, he went to work in a dry-goods store in Boston. Boys did the work then that a janitor might do now. Before breakfast, Edward opened the store and swept the floors. In winter he made the fires. After breakfast he packed or unpacked cases of goods. There were no typewriters so he copied out letters in a letter book by hand. That was, he said, how he learned to write business letters. He thought boys who went to work in this way got something they never learned in school. He called it gumption. Apparently it was a good kind of training because he became a successful and useful businessman, first as a textile expert, then as a pioneer in protecting textile mills against fire, and later in fire insurance.

How he traveled to his work in Boston for the first two years, he does not say. Perhaps he walked. Many people still walked into town over the Mill Dam. After 1844 however he could have taken the train, for the great event of that year in Brookline was that the railroad came to town.

The first train to Brookline was drawn by a special engine, gaily painted with red and gold and with BROOK-LINE on the side in large letters. The first day it came everyone rode free and it soon became the fashionable way to travel. Of course there were people who criticized the trains. One man wrote that he saw no reason for hurrying to New York uncomfortably in two days when you could go comfortably by stagecoach in ten. What

there was comfortable about traveling by stagecoach is
hard to say. Travelers got up at dawn in summer and
earlier in winter, they froze or broiled all day according

to the weather, they breathed dust sometimes and at
others had to get out and walk uphill in the mud so that
the horses could pull the coach. They stopped at inns
where the food was often poor and the beds neither clean
nor comfortable. No wonder most people soon changed
to traveling by train.

No one in town realized how much the puffing little
Brookline engine was going to change things. When it
made its first trip, Brookline was a quiet country town of
farms and market gardens. It was also a summer resort for
Boston people, who packed up and moved out in their
chaises as people now do when they put the electric mixer
and other treasures into their cars and move to Cohasset
or Annisquam. In 1844 there were only fifteen miles of
public roads in Brookline. Three years before, a committee had been appointed to name them. Most of the
names are still familiar: Boylston, Walnut, Warren, Cottage, Clyde, Newton, Washington, Harvard, School, Cypress, Hammond. Cross Street was the old name for

Hammond Street. What we now call Chestnut Hill Avenue was originally Brighton Street.

Also there were, of course, little grass-grown lanes leading to farms and there were small roads, not yet accepted by the town, which led off the larger streets. In all the Longwood section of Brookline there was not yet a single public highway.

The same year the railroad came, the town took over a part of Roxbury which was between where High Street now runs and Muddy River and the ponds that flow into it. The addition of this piece of old Roxbury brought the area of Brookline up to 4695 acres. There were two hundred and twelve dwellings in town and the population was 1682. By using long division — with which I had plently of trouble in my school days — I find that the average house had more than twenty-two acres of land around it and about eight people living in it.

Let's take a look at the schools in Brookline when Edward Atkinson was a boy. You remember when I showed you the old Putterham school the other day? You thought it looked pretty small, even for a country schoolhouse. I forgot to tell you that it was enlarged in 1839. Before that it was even smaller than the little yellow building you saw.

In 1842 the school committee made a report that the town of Brookline has taken pride in using as a standard ever since. It said that "the public schools of this town ought not to be inferior to those of any town in the Commonwealth." The first step in improving the school system was to plan a High School, which was organized in

1843 for children over ten years old. Two years later intermediate schools were started. Music was taught in the schools for the first time in 1844. It was started with the idea of "softening the hearts of the pupils." How well this worked no one says. Perhaps they were not very hard to start with.

Brookline had its first public library in 1857. For some years there had been a private library which circulated books among its members and in 1846 there was a room full of books where the members could meet and read. This library was disbanded for a strange reason. Out in California gold was discovered. In 1849 Brookline readers put down their books, exchanged them for picks and shovels, and rushed out to California to dig for gold. A glance at the catalogue of the old library society makes me think that the members may have been yawning over their books. No doubt there were nuggets of golden wisdom in these volumes of ancient sermons and in the books on law and philosophy but digging for real gold nuggets in the open air must have been fun for a change.

While prospectors were digging for gold in California, great changes were going on in Brookline. People were beginning to light their houses with gas instead of by candles and whale oil lamps. In 1853 the town ordered twenty street lamps and paid the Gaslight Company $25 a year for the gas. The lights were not lighted every night. On moonlight nights, the selectmen announced, the lamps would not burn.

In 1858 the first public sidewalk in town was laid. It was made of planks, such sturdy, well-seasoned timbers that a few of these old walks are still in existence. Brookline had a tradition of doing things well if they were to be done at all and the sidewalks were built on the principle that a good sidewalk must protect the walkers from mud at all seasons of the year.

"So they had mud time in Brookline then," Andrew commented.

"Yes," his grandmother said, "but the sidewalks really kept people's feet dry."

About this same time — she added — the first speed limit was set for Brookline traffic. It was forbidden to drive a horse faster than eight miles an hour. A horse going at a good fast trot will travel ten miles an hour so I am afraid the traffic laws must have been broken about as soon as they were made.

"Didn't fire engines go faster than that?" asked Susie.

"Yes, when they were drawn by horses, but in Edward Atkinson's boyhood they were still hauled by hand. In 1828 a new engine was bought and an engine house for Roxbury and Brookline was built on Washington Street. New buckets and hose were bought in 1829 and ten years later a hook and ladder. The bell on the Baptist Church was used to call the firemen together. The company disbanded when their own engine house was burned in 1843. However, a new company was formed in 1846.

Brookline may not have had bright lights on its streets, especially on moonlight nights, but it had music. When Edward Atkinson was not copying out business letters and unpacking cases of dry goods, he was arranging concerts. There were band concerts, sometimes on Linden

Place, sometimes on the triangle near the First Parish Church. There was a Mendelssohn Quintet, which Edward helped to organize and which played together for almost half a century. He got up dancing parties — sociables, they were called — with one or two pieces of music. The young men came, he says, in frock coats and they wore cotton gloves. Most of them did not own dress suits and kid gloves. It is safe to say that they would have been surprised to learn that a hundred years later they could have hired complete outfits from a shop not far from where they were dancing.

The refreshments at these dances were apples, lemonade, and cake. Older people had more formal parties in the Lyceum Hall. There would be, Edward wrote, a long table spread in the room above it with quite a little feast of a supper. He always loved parties and he gave some of the pleasantest ones I ever went to.

"You went to his parties!" Susie exclaimed. "Why, Grandma — you're not a hundred years old!"

"Not quite," her grandmother admitted, "but you know your best friends don't have to be exactly your own age. It's true that Mr. Atkinson was fifty-nine years older than I and I am lucky enough to have some friends who are more than fifty-nine years younger than I am. I always thought of him as a friend and when the tenth of February came around every year — that was his birthday — I knew I would be asked to the party he always gave for his grandchildren and the other children in the neighborhood. For me that was the greatest day in the year."

"What happened at those parties?" Andrew asked.

Sometimes, his grandmother told him, there was a magician, who took a rabbit out of his tall black silk hat when we were perfectly sure the hat was empty. He found fifty-cent pieces in little boys' ears. He would make a silk handkerchief disappear and when he pulled it out of the air again, there would be five more handkerchiefs, all different colors, tied to it. Sometimes there was a magic-lantern show. Wonderful colored pictures of castles and knights in armor and beautiful princesses would come on the screen and then fade away. We would play games — Hunt the Slipper and London Bridge. London Bridge would end with two lines swaying back and forth and falling. There would be a great heap of girls in embroidered muslin with wonderful sashes, girls in pink or pale blue silk or red velvet, boys in blue suits and stiff white colors, boys dressed like Little Lord Fauntleroy in black velvet and lace and red sashes, boys in white sailor suits. The ones in the Lord Fauntleroy suits usually behaved the worst but there was a certain amount of kicking by almost everyone.

After playing games and singing songs, we'd all go in to supper. Mr. Atkinson always sat at the head of the table. He was very handsome with beautiful silvery hair and beard, pink cheeks, and very bright eyes, blue, I think. I always confused him with Santa Claus but I also thought he must look like a king. I think that is because he once wore a gold paper crown that came out of a cracker. The crackers were wonderful. There are no crackers like them any more. They came from England.

They were about a foot and a half long, covered with silver and gold paper, and colored tissue paper, and pictures on top of that, and fringed at the ends. You pulled with the person sitting next to you and shut your eyes. After a minute of terror, there would be a loud crack from inside — ten times as loud as crackers sound now — and a smell of gunpowder. At least I thought it was gunpowder. Anyway it blew the wrappings of the cracker to pieces and you would find your hat. It might be a Roman emperor's helmet of purple and gold, or a clown's hat, or a bonnet with pink roses, or almost any other kind of hat you can imagine. Of course the boys wanted clowns' hats or soldiers' hats but they had to wear bonnets if they got them. Then there were presents inside — tiny metal fire engines or rings with bright red stones or watches that always said twenty minutes past eight. There was also poetry, remarkable poetry, and wise advice about the future. Really those crackers had everything — art, science, literature, prophecy, everything but food and that followed immediately.

It always tasted wonderful. There would be chicken sandwiches and ice cream and Mr. Atkinson's birthday cake with a whole forest of candles on it. Someone would tease him by asking him if it had been baked in his Aladdin Oven. This was the name of a fireless cooker he had invented. He called it his hay box. I suppose the original one must have been insulated with hay. To use it, he said, the cook must get something boiling hot — a ham, perhaps, and then shut it up in the cooker and leave it to cook slowly for a long time. Much of the heat would be kept in by the insulation and the ham would be tender and delicious.

Mr. Atkinson would be interested to know that the same principle is still used in many ways. You use it when you fill a thermos bottle or if you cook in an insulated electric oven. When you see the light switch off on an electric roaster, it means that the insulation is keeping the roaster at the temperature where you set the control. The fuel used is different and the thermostat is new but the idea of insulation is really his.

"I wish I could bake him a cake in my electric roaster," she added.

"How old would he be now?" asked Andrew.

"You do the arithmetic," she suggested. "You are the mathematician around here."

"Is a hundred and twenty-eight years all right for 1955?"

"It sounds all right."

"What a lot of candles!" said Susie.

"Then," Andrew went on, "it's as if you could remember back more than a hundred years and if I remember what you say, it's as if I could."

"Yes, because Edward Atkinson did what I hope you'll do sometime. He wrote down what he remembered. And through his memory we can go back still farther — to Miss Dana who remembered the Revolution, to the spire of the old meetinghouse, from which you could look out over Boston Harbor and see the masts of ships that had come from Russia and from China around the Horn, to

Dr. Pierce, walking eight miles to preach and home again. I think I'll stop this evening with a story that Edward Atkinson told about Dr. Pierce.

"When Dr. Pierce died there was no doubt in the mind of anyone in Brookline that he would go to Heaven. And they say that he did and that when he got to the heavenly gates, St. Peter welcomed him kindly and said, 'Isn't this Dr. Pierce?'

"And Dr. Pierce took out his big old fashioned watch, looked at it and said, 'Yes, just twenty minutes from Brookline, and walked all the way!' "

Susie was interested in the next thing that had come out of the trunk, a pair of white satin slippers, square-toed, with flat heels. There was also an old fan with ivory sticks. The fan part was made from an old colored engraving. It showed the wall of a grand mansion. You could see the house through the open iron gate in a high stone wall. Green trees hung their branches over the wall and almost hid a river and a church spire in the distance. A piratical-looking man with his head tied up in a handkerchief, a cloak, and a black slouch hat was leaning on a box, which was resting on a frame. He had a small boy with him who was beating a drum. The sound of the drum had called some gaily dressed ladies from the big house and one of them was looking through a glass circle in the side of the box.

"What is this?" asked Andrew, "Television?"

"It's as much like television as anything they had a

hundred and fifty years ago," his grandmother told him.
"We've moved back to 1800 now and that box is a traveling peep show. They looked through that little window
and saw whatever was inside — perhaps a harbor with
ships, a castle attacked by knights in armor, or a ballroom
where dancers were doing the minuet."

"I wonder what was inside this one," said Susie.

"That's something we'll never know," her grandmother
said.

"Do you know whose the slippers were?" Susie asked.

"Yes, they were the slippers your great-great-grandmother Wilder wore at her wedding."

"Why, they aren't big enough for me!" Susie said.
"What else did she wear to the wedding and what was it
like?"

"I wish I knew but I have a letter here that tells about
another wedding of about the same time. It was in 1809,
the wedding of Mary Goddard and Samuel May," her
grandmother said.

"That looks like your writing," said Andrew. "Did
they write like that in 1809?"

"It is my writing — I copied the original letter, which
is in the Brookline Public Library. I've shortened it, but
only a little. Shall I read it to you?"

"Yes, please," he said, "unless of course you have
trouble reading your writing," he added kindly and with
a gleam in his eyes familiar to his grandmother. She
passed over this well-worn family joke by saying that it
would really be no trouble at all and started reading the
letter.

My dear sister —

Mary desired me to write you all about last Wednesday
— and without any more preamble I will begin. We, Pa,
Ma, Brother G. and myself, went to the wedding house
about seven o'clock and before 8 I believe the company
were all there. Our grandmother and her seven daughters,
Mrs. Joseph Goddard with ten children, all our uncles,
Brothers Henry and John, Messers Holly, Emerson and
Pierce with their ladies, Mr. and Mrs. Nathaniel Goddard
with four children and two of Uncle Sam's apprentices,
making fifty-five in all.

The bride did not appear until all the company arrived when our uncle led her in. Cousin John F. followed
with Sister S. and Brother G. and L. Archbold. They took
their proper stations, the Bride and Groom under or
before the looking glass at the back of the room. Mr.
Holly performed the ceremony. Mr. Emerson made the
prayer and Mr. Pierce read an appropriate hymn, which
was sung by all the company to the tune of St. Martin's.

The bride was dressed in white satin with a veil thrown
over her head. Sister S. wore her white muslin dress and
to do her justice she never looked so handsome before.
Mrs. Holly was the most beautiful woman in the room.
At about half past nine the company went in to supper.
Oh, sister, it is more than I can do to tell you half how
elegant the supper was. You ought to have seen it. The
table was laid from one corner of the room to the other,
leaving just room for the servants to pass, in the middle
of the table was a cake made I can't tell you how. It was
large and thick and upon it there seemed to be another of

a smaller size and upon that a Temple built of light con-
fectionary. There were in it priests and priestesses, two
doves and a nest and on top a bird just ready to fly with
this couplet in his mouth. "May love, may health, may
happiness be thine," Oh dear I have forgot the other line,
it was something about "honestly combine." Sister S.
read it aloud at Mr. Emerson's request. At each end of the
table was a cake elegantly dressed, very differently from
yours, I do assure you. The frosting although put on
very smooth did not look as thick and it was not dressed
with almonds, plums and caraway seeds, but with the fine
mustard seed as it is called, strawberries, peaches, and
limes that were very elegantly made rough with a kind
of frosting. So much for the cake. Now for the rest of
the good things, which were in great abundance. Cold
meats of every kind, indeed there was nothing hot but
the chicken pye, fruits of all kinds that the season affords,
custards, whips and trifles, ice creams, in short everything
you can name of the best kind.

The company separated before twelve and the bride
with her husband attended by the bridesmaids went to
their house on Purchase Street and next day set off on a
journey to Connecticut in a carriage with four horses
and there we must leave them for the present.

Your affectionate sister MARY

"Who were the Goddards?" asked Susie. "Were they
related to us?"

"No, but they were friends and neighbors for many
years," her grandmother said.

They were like a great many families of the time — she went on — but we know more about them because luckily they wrote letters and diaries and saved them. This notebook — in some more of my handwriting, Andrew — is full of copies of Goddard letters and of parts of Benjamin Goddard's diaries. I made the copies when I first planned this book. The diaries are homemade books, bound in pieces of old wallpapers, left over, I suppose, when the Goddard house was papered. In them Benjamin Goddard tells about what he is planting on his farm, what crops he takes to market, what books he is reading, what he thinks of the administration in Washington (he thinks they are scoundrels) , and about evenings of music with his family and friends.

The letters are written by Mrs. Benjamin Goddard to her niece, Mrs. Samuel Goddard, in England. Mrs. Samuel, before she married, was Mehitable Dawes. You'll remember, her father was William Dawes, who rode out through Boston and Brookline on the night of the eighteenth of April, 1775, to warn the countryside that the British would soon be on their way to capture the military stores at Concord. Mehitable used to tell her children about it. She used to tell them too about how she used to stay, sometimes for a year at a time, with her aunt and uncle in Brookline. She thought the house and the country around it the most beautiful place to live in the world. The house was the fine old square yellow house that I showed you the other day. Here is a picture of it before it was moved to Sumner Road where it now stands. It used to face the turnpike with a wide green meadow in front

of it. It is still on a piece of land that used to be part of
Benjamin Goddard's farm.

The Benjamin Goddards had no children of their own.
Instead they used to have nieces and nephews for long
visits. One nephew who used to come to stay was Samuel
Goddard. He lived in Portsmouth, New Hampshire, but
he had two grandfathers in Brookline — Mr. Heath on
Heath Hill and Mr. Goddard on Goddard Avenue. He
used to visit his Grandfather Heath or his Uncle Benjamin and while he was staying at either house, he would
walk through woods and fields and green lanes to his
Grandfather Goddard's house.

This walk took him past what he thought was the most
beautiful house in the world. It is still standing at the
corner of Cottage and Warren Streets, a white house with
a two-story porch supported by slender columns. It was
called Green Hill and when Samuel used to stop there on
his way to his grandfather's, it was owned by a lady known
as Madam Babcock. She was a very wonderful person in
the eyes of the small boys and girls who used to come
and see her. She was always beautifully dressed, sitting in
a chair in her upper sitting room with her cane beside her.
She loved flowers and birds and children. The house was
surrounded by lilacs as tall as trees, by fragrant syringas,
and double-flowered cherries. There were great beds of
tulips and narcissus. The flower beds were watered and
weeded. Birds were fed and protected from cats. Children were kindly and graciously welcomed.

After they had been sitting quietly for some time,
Madam Babcock would reach out with her cane and tap

gently at a certain place on the wall. This was a magic signal, Samuel thought. In a few moments the door would open and in would come Green, the old man-servant, carrying a tray. On the tray would be delicious things to eat, especially a kind of gingerbread that tasted different from any other gingerbread in the world.

Madam Babcock lived in Boston in the winter and it was a great day for the children when she moved out to Brookline for the summer. Her coach had a high box in front, on which the coachman sat. At the back was a plat-form on which Green always stood. He kept his balance as they rolled along through Roxbury, past the Punch Bowl and up Walnut Street, by grasping two long leather straps attached to the back of the coach.

Samuel always was one of Madam Babcock's early visi-tors. He liked walking past the wide beds full of bright flowers, over the smoothly spread red gravel, and up onto the shady porch with the woodbine twisting around the high pillars. Inside he liked the little flight of stairs that led down into the great parlor. When he got into the parlor, it seemed as if he had sailed away to a foreign country. On the walls was a paper showing scenes along a wide river with curiously shaped boats, buildings with domes and towers, and people in strange clothes. The whole thing was in rich, brilliant colors even when I saw it at least a hundred years later and is so even now, I suppose.

Madam Babcock told Samuel that the design on the paper was called The Banks of the Bosphorus. He used to look at the sails and the towers and the trees and think,

If I were only rich enough, I would have a house just like this. Perhaps if I go away overseas I shall make my fortune . . .

Samuel grew up into a tall, strong young man with reddish hair. He looked very handsome to his small cousin Mehitable, especially when he was playing battledore and shuttlecock. One day she counted how many times he bounced the shuttlecock into the air without ever letting it touch the ground and it was 1046 times. Everyone thought it was wonderful but no one was as excited as Mehitable. Perhaps that was why her Cousin Sam finally noticed her. Anyway he did and when she was only seventeen, they were married.

Samuel still had the idea of going overseas to make his fortune and they soon sailed across the Atlantic where he went into business in Manchester, England. Mehitable must have been glad to get her aunt's letters from Brookline, for she saved them and brought them back with her many years later. Mrs. Goddard always kept track of the sailing dates and would send a letter, not through the post office, but by the captain of the ship or by one of the passengers. She numbered her letters throughout the year, beginning over again with number one each January. This was done so that Mehitable would know if all the letters reached her. Once it took forty-four days for the letter to reach Liverpool, so naturally it took a long time for an answer. Luckily the news in the letters was welcome even if it was not exactly fresh. Mehitable was glad to get it because it told exactly the things she wanted to know. There was news about the family weddings, about new babies and boys in school and college, about the health and sickness of her friends. Unluckily it was mostly sickness. Typhoid fever, tuberculosis, and other kinds of fevers were common. The letters brought the news of many deaths, often of young people, from these causes. It had not yet occurred to anyone that such illness might be prevented. The favorite treatment was to take blood from the sick person's veins, to put a mustard plaster on his chest, and to give various violent medicines which were nothing more nor less than poisons. Sometimes people — tough ones — got well in spite of these methods.

Love for Brookline runs all through the letters. Every spring seems more beautiful than the one before it. Sometimes it is late, sometimes it is early, but the flowering of cherry, peach, pear, and apple trees and the brilliant green grass are always welcome. The Goddards have oval flower beds, which in May are in "great pride" with tulips, narcissus, and peonies. There are many dandelions in the fields and asparagus and radishes in the garden.

One spring when Mrs. Goddard wrote, the ladies of the First Parish were especially busy. They had decided that Dr. Pierce, their much loved minister, needed a new gown to wear in the pulpit. They collected ninety dollars and since this was more than was needed for the gown, they also bought him shirts, a new neck cloth, and gloves.

"Was not that a good thing?" Mrs. Goddard asked Mehitable.

The building where Dr. Pierce wore his new gown was almost square — sixty-eight by sixty-four feet with a wide

porch in front. The main part of the church was thirty-
five feet, six inches high from the foundation to the eaves.
The spire was one hundred and thirty-seven feet from the
ground. You could climb it — if you were a small boy —
and see the masts of the ships in Boston Harbor.

In this building there were seventy-four pews downstairs and fourteen in the gallery. The caps of the pews
and the pulpit were made of southern cherry wood. The
building and furnishing of the church cost about $20,000,
which was raised by selling the pews at auction. The
prices ranged from a hundred and twenty-five dollars for
a seat in the gallery to five hundred and twenty-five dollars for a pew on the floor, with the privilege of choosing
it. One upholstered pew, Mr. David Hyslop's, was regarded as very luxurious and distinguished. Children admired the soft cushions, the red morocco hymnbooks with
the Hyslop arms on them and the special drawer made to
hold them.

Mr. Hyslop was distinguished more for the outside of
his hymnbooks than for any ability to use the inside of
them. He was completely without an ear for music. A
visiting minister, who did not know Mr. Hyslop, once
quoted in his sermon Shakespeare's lines about music:

> *The man who has no music in himself*
> *Nor is not moved with concord of sweet sounds*
> *Is fit for treasons, stratagems and spoils.*

Mr. Hyslop took this poetry as a personal insult. He
put away his scarlet hymnbook, left his cushioned pew,

and walked deliberately out of the church. He disliked music so much that he called anthems "tantrums" and he refused to go to church on Thanksgiving Day because there were likely to be "tantrums" in the service.

Mr. Hyslop was almost hideously ugly. He was lame and he had never learned to talk as plainly as a small child can speak. He had never received much education but he had inherited what was in those days a large fortune and what was then — and still is — one of the finest houses in Brookline. It is the old Boylston house, the yellow house, high on Fisher Hill, facing the Worcester Turnpike and the Reservoir.

Daily life with Mr. Hyslop must have been difficult because of some of his strange ideas. He had a small dark room on the third story of the house, which he called his "iron study." He pronounced it "tudy" as he had trouble in saying the letter S. In this secret place he hid all the pieces of iron and other metals he could find, sometimes kettles, porringers, and skillets that were in use in the kitchen.

He kept the room locked up. Often when he was asked about an iron spoon, or even a silver one, that had been missing for weeks, he would calmly produce the key and return the missing object. A rake or a peel — the long-handled shovel for taking bread out of the brick oven — or a horse's halter: all might vanish into the "iron tudy."

Every member of the household had to be present before breakfast while the master prayed. He kept his eyes opened and often mentioned in his imperfect speech things he happened to notice. Once his pet monkey started to investigate a pan of sausage which the cook had left frying on the fire when she came in to prayers. To her surprise part of the prayer was: "Hetty, keep the monkey out of the frying pan."

Beautiful fruit trees of all kinds grew on the Hyslop place. There was far more fruit than the family could possibly eat but Mr. Hyslop would neither sell it nor give it away. Great piles of it lay rotting under the trees every year. This must have made the orchard a depressing sight in the fall but in spring when all the trees were in bloom, no place looked lovelier.

Spring was, of course, an especially busy time in Brookline as it is in all farming towns. The busiest time of all, however, was not connected with farming — it was Election week. It had nothing to do with voting for town officers either but was part of the church year. For several days there were meetings of ministers, there were sermons and suppers — and what suppers!

The ladies of the parish did their best baking. They got out their cook books, which told how to make cake with eighteen eggs and two pounds of butter, and got to work. There was a special kind of cake called Election Cake.

"It sounds like something you might make," Susie said.

"Well," said her grandmother, "if mine tastes half as good to you as my grandmother's Election Cake did to me, I'm delighted. It was a kind of fruit cake, very good but no better than that angel cake you made for my birthday, Andrew. I don't suppose there are many people who have cake made for their birthdays both by their grandmothers and their grandsons, do you?"

Men always make good cooks when they put their minds on it — she went on. Edward Atkinson began his cooking, long before he invented his fireless cooker, by pounding up spices for his mother when she was going to bake a cake. Spices came whole then, instead of ground up in packages. They all had to be pounded fine except nutmeg. Nutmeg was grated. I used to do it for my grandmother on a little tin grater. It had a box at the top just big enough to hold one nutmeg. I didn't have to pound sugar though. It came granulated, but when Mehitable Dawes lived in Brookline, it came in a loaf, a sort of rounded pyramid. The children of the family had the task of breaking off pieces and pounding them up in a mortar with a pestle.

The ladies of the house in early Brookline days oversaw whatever work was going on and did a great deal of it themselves. They were up before six in the morning and, after bathing in cold water, they put on crisp, fresh calico dresses with white collars and cuffs and were ready to see about breakfast. There were likely to be visitors in these big hospitable farmhouses, so, with the hired men and girls, there was always a big group around the table.

Breakfast was a hearty meal. It needed to be, because on a farm the men had already put in hours of work before they sat down.

"What would they have?" asked Andrew.

Perhaps a broiled steak — his grandmother told him. It was usually tough and one of the breakfast-time sounds would be the pounding of steak to make it tender enough to eat. They didn't make hamburg out of it because meat grinders hadn't been invented yet. Chops or fish of different kinds were served for breakfast too. Sometimes ham or bacon and eggs. Corned beef hash or fish hash were favorites too. On Sundays there would be fish balls with baked beans and brown bread left over from Saturday night supper. In most houses a brick oven was part of the kitchen fireplace. When the cook wanted to use the oven, she first made a fire in it and let it burn till the oven was good and hot. Then she quickly cleaned out the ashes and any live coals and put in her cakes and pie, shut it up quickly again, and left it alone until the right time.

"How did they know when that was?" Susie asked.

Her grandmother said she supposed they must have known by instinct because no one had timers or oven thermometers or thermostats. The heat from the rest of the fireplace kept the oven from cooling off too fast, she said, and made an even temperature. Wonderful things to eat came out of those brick ovens.

Broiling was done over the coals in the fireplace. For roasting there was what was called a tin kitchen, a sort of reflecting oven that stood in front of the fire. The big crane in the fireplace would hold several kettles in which things could be boiled. Frying pans had handles almost as long as you are tall, Andrew, she said, so the cook wouldn't be scorched and stifled with smoke while she was cooking the ham and eggs. All this cooking was a very smoky business and managing a fire so as to get the most heat and the least smoke was an art in itself.

After a while the Goddards had a wonderful improvement in their Brookline house. It was called a Rumford Roaster, after its inventor, Benjamin Thompson, Count Rumford. It consisted of a collection of ovens that were heated centrally instead of having fires in them. Brookline neighbors were much excited about this modern way of cooking and thought the dinners that came out of the new ovens were wonderfully good.

There would probably be a big roast of beef or pork with vegetables from their own garden. Mr. Goddard raised vegetables for the Boston market and his diaries tell about his planting peas and beans and carrots and corn. Sometimes they had roast chicken or chicken pie and there would be freshly baked bread with butter churned from their own cream. For dessert, two or three kinds of pie. One kind would always be made of their own apples, either fresh or dried according to the season. There might be a steamed pudding with sauce like yellow foam.

Tea was the last meal of the day. In some families they drank coffee but tea was more usual. With it they had thin bread and butter, cold tongue or ham, sponge cake or pound cake, and some sort of preserves such as apple-sauce or brandied peaches. If company came in the evening, they were offered lemonade and cake in summer and in winter, cider, apples, nuts, and raisins.

All the girls in a family, daughters, nieces, visitors, bound girls, hired girls, would help with the cooking. One would make the bread, another the pies. Cake would be the specialty of one and doughnuts of another. One might keep the silver and brasses bright while another polished the pewter. The mother of the family usually washed the fine china herself. Two small tin tubs of hot water would be set on trays on the dining-room table. She would put on her everyday apron over her best embroidered black satin apron — like this one here, Susie, of your great-great-grandmother's — roll up her embroidered muslin cuffs and go to work.

Mehitable Goddard was always interested in the fashions and in one letter her aunt described what the girls were wearing: "Black beaver hats with very little brim, full of feathers with a gold band — very tasty." One of them had "a new crimson coat, trimmed full with velvet" and one of Mehitable's cousins appeared at a recent party in Boston in "a light striped purple pelisse, very dressy and handsome, with last year's beaver hat." Mrs. Goddard herself wore a black twilled silk edged with velvet to the party.

The journey to Boston was regarded as quite an undertaking and she writes that she felt happy to return to the calm, quiet house.

"Here," she said, "I can read and think; don't see how Boston folks can do either."

Land journeys, the trip to Boston by way of Roxbury and Boston Neck, were hard work. Yet Boston men sailed their ships to every port in the world as naturally as we might take a train for New York. They traveled to so many ports that in China, and other distant places, all Americans were called Bostonians. Ocean travel then was really easier than journeys by land.

Mr. Goddard bought a new chaise but he did not like going into Boston any better than his wife did so they seldom drove in that direction. The Worcester Turnpike had recently been built and they could drive along it and call on the Heaths or the Hyslops. On Sundays they drove to the meetinghouse. There were no automobile accidents on the quiet Brookline roads because there were no automobiles, but there were dangers of a different kind. The last day of April in 1825, Mrs. Goddard took her niece Louisa for a drive. This drive was for Louisa's health but it turned out unfortunately.

"Our horse started," Mrs. Goddard wrote, "broke the whiffletree, which caused him to run, and threw us with great violence from the chaise. Louisa was only slightly scratched and bruised but I was taken up senseless. Dr. Wild was sent for. Blood was taken in plenty. My collar bone was broken and my left arm and whole side much strained and bruised. My arm is very weak and lame yet.

Were it the right side it would be a far greater incon-
venience. I never had much courage about driving and
shall have less than ever. We have the same long tailed
blacky that you may remember. He is subject to inequali-
ties of spirits and unlike his master is governed by his
feelings."

Although she had the best doctors available, her arm
never really got well again. Apparently the collarbone
was not properly set. With no X-rays, it was not possible
to see what was the trouble. It was broken by the doctor
and reset some months later but this painful operation,
performed without anesthetics of course, didn't improve
it much. A broken bone was much more serious then than
now. One strange example of what might happen to a
break, if the injured person had no medical care, was
brought to light with the finding of the skeleton of an
Indian. It was discovered when some grading was being
done near the corner of Walnut and Chestnut Streets for
an addition to the burying ground. At some time one
of his legs had been broken and never set. One end of the
broken bone had lapped past the other and they had
grown together in a way to make that leg some inches
shorter than the other. The poor man must have hobbled
painfully through the rest of his life.

How long it has been since this lame Indian limped
over the old Sherburne Trail, no one knows, but Walnut
Street still follows the old curves of this ancient footpath
made by Indians striding along it. One of these curves
takes you around the great boulder where the Wishing
Stone is.

There has been traffic along this highway for more than three hundred years — when it was a footpath in the wilderness, when it was just wide enough for a horse and rider, when men walked beside the ox teams that carried their wives, their children, and their household goods west, when people rode to meeting in their chaises. Even stagecoaches used to pass the Wishing Stone and the meetinghouse and the triangular green that was the center of the town.

The men who laid out the Worcester Turnpike knew that a straight line is the shortest distance between two points and they made the turnpike as straight as they could, paying no attention to the hills between Boston and Worcester. Some of the hills were so steep that the horses could hardly drag the heavy coaches up the grades. The men passengers and sometimes the women would have to get out and walk uphill to spare the horses. It would have been better engineering and the journey would have taken less time if the road had followed some of the valleys at the foot of the hills. One of these steep hills, called Walley's Hill, lay between the Benjamin Goddards' house and Boston. It was so steep that for some time after the turnpike was built, in 1806, the stagecoaches turned off at the Punch Bowl Village and followed Walnut Street up past the meetinghouse and joined the turnpike again near what is now the corner of Sumner Road.

At last the hill was cut down. Mrs. Goddard was very pleased about it and wrote to Mehitable that "Uncle and neighbors are much engaged in digging down Walley's Hill. Since the opening of the new avenue to Boston [the

Mill Dam] this was the only hill between us and Beacon Hill and it was always hard to mount it. Your Uncle has been much engaged in representing the importance of the object and has obtained four or five hundred dollars toward it. You must come home and see for I cannot tell you half how delightful it is to ride to Boston without any rough road, any hills, on pavement. Lest you may not feel at home when you first come in, I will have nothing done to your little chamber, though the azure is almost worn from the floor, otherwise it is just as you left it."

Although there was beginning to be a good deal of travel along the turnpike, the Goddards still lived on a quiet farm. Theirs was the only house on their side of the road until the traveler came to the edge of the Punch Bowl Village, as Brookline Village was called even in distant parts of Vermont and New Hampshire and indeed in any place from which men drove cattle to Boston.

The Punch Bowl Village must have been at its pleasantest at this time. The original part of the tavern, a square, hip-roofed building, painted yellow, had been built before 1740, and had been enlarged so many times by moving other buildings and joining them to it that the whole collection — the many kinds of roofs, doorways, and windows, the many sizes and shapes and colors — made it seem to Brookline people rather like that strange rocky mixture, their native pudding stone. The tavern buildings, and indeed the whole village, were shaded by great elms and Lombardy poplars, and buttonwoods. These buttonwoods were sycamores with white patches of bark on their trunks and fruit like little balls.

The cattle always stopped to drink the clear water of the ford near the tavern. Close by, where the railway tracks now run, the brook spread out. Barefooted boys herded cattle through the stream or stopped to fish from the cart bridge. From the bowling green came the click of bowls. The old tavern sign on its red post creaked in the wind. Brookline people were proud of that sign with its generous painted bowl of Chinese porcelain, its big ladle, and the lemon tree above it. The tree hung so heavy with fruit that some lemons had fallen and were lying on the table beside the bowl as if ready to be cut when some more of the famous punch was mixed.

In front of the tavern was a long bench where visitors could sit and watch the yellow stagecoach come swinging up to the door with little puffs of dust rising from the horses' hoofs and a cloud of dust shining in the sunlight. This was a modern and very swift coach. When the weather was good and if the passengers walked up the steepest hills, it could reach New York in six days.

After 1821 the coaches could drive right into Boston over the Mill Dam instead of following the twisting road over the narrow neck of land that connected the peninsula of Boston with less important parts of the United States. The Mill Dam roads, there were three of them, were built partly with the idea of using the force of the tides to run mills, partly to make it possible to cross the tidal waters and the marshy fens of the Back Bay. The water-power project was not a success but the roads at once became useful — and are still so. The first branch of the Mill Dam was an extension of Beacon Street, beginning at

Charles Street and running out to Sewall's Point in Brookline, not far from where the Beacon Street subway cars now come out into the sunlight. The second branch, Commonwealth Avenue, joined Beacon Street at what we now call Kenmore Square. So did the third branch — Brookline Avenue. These streets all had open water along them at high tide and great expanses of mud at low tide. The roads made the journey to Boston easy but the tolls were considered expensive. There was a charge of 6¼ cents for a chaise to go to town by Brookline Avenue.

If you did not have a carriage of your own, you might travel to Boston by Eliphalet Spurr's stage, which ran from the Punch Bowl. It cost twenty-five cents each way. This price was so high that most people had to walk. There were plenty of women who would walk the four miles or more into Boston by Roxbury Neck, do their shopping and walk back again. Perhaps a small boy would go along and carry the bundles.

After they left the village, they might have a mile or two extra to walk. In hot weather Walnut Street, as people were beginning to call the Old Sherburne Trail, was the shadiest. In 1828 they might stop and see how the building of Mr. John Tappan's stone house was getting on. Mr. Tappan was proud of his unusual house — later the Philbrick house where a certain red petticoat sometimes hung on the line. Brookline houses were of wood, less commonly of brick, and a stone house was a novelty. Mr. Tappan's house also had the distinction of being the one hundredth house in town.

Even after the Mill Dam was built there was no bridge

across the Charles River in Boston. To travel either north or west by land it was necessary to go through the Punch Bowl Village. Stores in northern Vermont were stocked with goods brought from Boston by ox team. Some of the time the oxen would travel over blazed trails, sometimes over muddy roads where a bridge over a stream would be only a few logs and planks, or perhaps no bridge at all, just a ford to splash through. They must have been glad when they reached the Punch Bowl Village and saw that the sign was still there with the bowl and the lemon tree hanging over it. One of the things they used to take back to Vermont with them was lemons. They also carried what were called West India goods — sugar, rum, and molasses. Tea from China, cottons from India, cups and saucers from England, all would be packed on the ox team. Here's an old sugar bowl from Vermont that went there by ox team so we know that it must have gone through the Punch Bowl Village a hundred and fifty years ago.

"I would like to have been in the village to see the ox teams go through," said Andrew.

"So would I," said his grandmother. "Would you like to know the day I would be in the village if I could choose?"

Andrew and Susie both said that they would.

"It would be the twenty-ninth of July, 1825."

"Why is that so special?"

"Because Marie Joseph Paul Yves Roche Gilbert du Motier, Marquis de Lafayette, was passing through. He wasn't any longer the gay young soldier who came to help

us in the Revolution and he looked, I suppose, in 1825
rather old. On the seventeenth of June, the anniversary
of the Battle of Bunker Hill, there was a great celebration.
Mrs. Goddard wrote to Mehitable: "There was a great
show on the seventeenth. Perhaps the greatest number of
people ever in Boston. Lafayette added greatly to the interest of the occasion. I saw the tables on Bunker Hill at
which four thousand people sat down to dine . . ."

"Lafayette visited towns and cities all through the thirteen colonies that he had helped to make into thirteen
states and he visited the fourteenth state too."

"You mean he was in Vermont?" Susie asked.

Yes — her grandmother said — he was in Montpelier.
And wherever he went, boys in their best blue suits and
white shirts and red, white and blue ribbons and girls in
white dresses with bouquets of white and red roses, tied
with blue ribbons, were there to welcome him. The boys
cheered and the girls threw flowers under his horse's feet.
Every now and then some little girl would be chosen to
give him a bouquet and a poem and he would thank her
and kiss her. I once knew an old lady in Brookline who
had been kissed by Lafayette. I never knew anything else
about her — except that she had caraway seed cookies,
which were good if you liked them. I didn't.

The Brookline that Lafayette rode through was a small
village surrounded by wooded hills, swamps and widely
scattered farms. Each one of these farms was like a small
factory. Almost everything a family needed was grown
there. They had their own beef, lamb, and chickens.
Their own wheat and corn were ground at the gristmill.

Their shoes were made from the hides of their own cattle, their clothes from the wool of their own sheep. If they built a new barn, they used their own timber and it rested on a foundation of stones from their own fields. They made the paint for it by stirring up Venetian red and skim milk. Many farmers made their own bricks for chimneys and fireplaces.

The women were as busy as the men. They spun and dyed wool, of course, but first they had to make the dyes and the soap for washing the wool. They made their own bread, including the yeast that raised it. At hog-killing time, they made sausage and pickled the bacon and hams that were hung in the smokehouses. Naturally they made the beds. Women still do. These women, however, first wove the sheets and the blankets. They made the mattresses and the pillows out of feathers from their own geese. In their spare time they made patchwork quilts.

"What spare time?" Susie inquired. "They sound busier than the men."

"Women often think that — for some reason," said her grandmother.

But — she went on — to do the men credit, the farmers of Brookline really fed the people of Boston. Cheese and butter, great baskets of ripe cherries and peaches and apples, fresh and smoked meats, asparagus and early peas were all carried into Boston. They might be sold for cash but in many cases they were exchanged for things needed on the farms.

You were looking at that old account book of your great-great-great-grandfather's, Andrew. It shows a good deal about how business was carried on. He was a farmer but he was also a doctor and a lawyer. All three professions are pretty well mixed up in the book. When he sells cider, he often takes his pay in the use of oxen for plowing one of his fields. He may pay for a roast of pork by drawing a will or setting a leg. Cash was scarce for a long time after the Revolution and the War of 1812. The system called Country Pay, in which no money changed hands, was the way most business was carried on. Men might pay their taxes by working on the roads with their ox teams. The blacksmith who shod their horses might be paid in corn meal or firewood or lumber or apples. Part of the minister's salary was paid in firewood. Brookline owned a special lot from which this wood was cut. Many young ministers were able to graduate from Harvard because their tuition could be paid in potatoes.

Most families, even if they were not farmers, raised a few vegetables and some fruit and kept a cow. Carpenters, painters, blacksmiths, cordwainers, or wheelwrights were all farmers too. Farmers ran the sawmills and the gristmills.

"What is a cordwainer?" Andrew asked.

"It used to mean a man who worked with a special kind of leather called cordovan and then it came to mean a shoemaker," his grandmother told him.

"Why didn't you say shoemaker?"

"Because I hoped you'd ask me and then I'd know if you were still awake."

When Lafayette went through the village — she went on — there were about nine hundred people in the town.

Half of them lived below the meetinghouse and half above. With the opening of the Mill Dam, the town began to change. It became so easy to drive in and out of Boston that the merchants from the city began to buy land in Brookline, build big comfortable houses and spend the summer there. The air was supposed to be better than the air of the city. There were still farms but the town was a summer resort too. These Boston merchants had vegetable gardens but they did not work in them except as a hobby.

For a while after the farms were turned into country estates, the houses still stood in large tracts of land. A Boston man spending his summer in Brookline could look from his own windows over land belonging to him, across the fens and marshes and patches of open water to the houses on Beacon Hill with the State House dome rising above them. On pleasant days he could see the harbor and perhaps one of his own ships coming into it.

From Heath Hill, where the Heaths built one house after another, you could catch a glimpse of the blue of the harbor, deeper than the blue of the sky. In 1813 Susan Heath painted a water color from her window. It showed the Back Bay at high tide and the State House. You could see somewhat the same view from Fisher Hill and at a different angle from Aspinwall Hill. From Corey Hill was the widest prospect of all.

There was less smoke hanging over Boston than there is now and it was easy to see the forest of masts along the wharves and the towering sails above them. Now, except on hot July afternoons when the east wind brings a breath of salty coolness across the city, we often forget that the sea is there. No one forgot it in the early nineteenth century. In the big families of those days there was almost always one boy who went to sea. When he came back, he brought some of the treasures that are still in Brookline houses.

There was the china for instance. Blue Canton was the commonest. As Brookline children ate their corned beef hash they could see the painted story on the plates. A rich mandarin had his ships in the harbor, his garden with its blossoming fruit trees. A bridge connected the mandarin's garden with a smaller garden and a cottage. In it lived the poor young man who was in love with the mandarin's daughter. He sang under her window and she heard him and ran away with him. Just as they were escaping across the bridge, her father caught them. The young man was killed and the girl died of a broken heart. A weeping willow hangs over their grave, but their souls turned into doves and flew in happy freedom around the sky.

Before dinner the children washed their hands in a bowl, also from China, painted with butterflies and birds and flowers. There might be goldfish on it too or ladies in long robes having tea in a Chinese garden. When the head of the family made punch on cold winter evenings, he might use a bright yellow bowl with blue and red dragons fighting among flowers. Serving guests at tea, a hostess could use her new tea set, ordered when her son set sail two years before and especially painted for her in Canton. It would have a design she had chosen, perhaps a blue border with stars on it and on the side a shield against folds of blue velvet lined with ermine. On the shield would be a flower or her initials, hard to read because they were all twined together, or the family coat of arms.

The Chinese were very careful and accurate about copying any design that was sent to them. One lady drew her pattern and underneath it wrote: "Put this in the middle." Two years later she got back her order — plates, platters, cups, saucers, tea pot, chocolate pot, sugar bowl, cream pitcher. Every single piece had her design on it just the way she had drawn it and underneath her coat of arms on every single one it said: "Put this in the middle."

Perhaps the ship from Boston went on to India and then the young sailor might bring his mother a shawl so light and soft that she could pull it through her wedding ring. Or perhaps the shawl would be heavy enough to keep out the cold winter winds that blew through the Punch Bowl Village when the sleigh bells were ringing. Its center might be scarlet or grass green or turquoise and around the edge a pattern in all sorts of colors. The shapes were not quite leaves and not quite flowers but the whole thing somehow reminded the sailor of a Brookline garden in spring. Perhaps he brought his father a set of red and white chessmen of carved ivory with three balls, one inside the other, that rattled in the base of each one. The knights rode chunky little horses and the kings and queens had slanting eyes and polite Oriental smiles. Yes, Andrew, like the ones in the cabinet. For his sisters there

would be carved ivory card cases, or jewel cabinets of
black and gold lacquer. The younger boys would have
packages of Chinese firecrackers wrapped in scarlet and
gold paper or Chinese kites painted with dragons to fly.
They flew them from Holden's Hill.

This hill was leveled long ago but it was the highest
point in the village once and there was always a breeze
there. The kites would tug at their strings and fly as high
as the steeple of the new Baptist Church, then higher,
higher, until even a Chinese boy couldn't have read the
Chinese characters on them. Holden's Hill was a good
place to set off your firecrackers too. You saved them for
Fourth of July.

The night before the Fourth, you thought you didn't
sleep at all and you really were awake now and then.
While it was still dark, you got up, gave your face what
was known as a "lick and a word of promise," stumbled
somehow into your clothes, and got to the hill in time to
be there when the cannon was fired. Every boy who had
waked in time was there too when the sky began to turn
pink. Birds were singing but soon you couldn't hear
them because the cannon began to rumble from higher
hilltops in Belmont and Watertown and Newton. Then
the Brookline one went off with a hoarse boom and a wonderful smell of burned powder. The firecrackers began
to snap and crackle. You broke one almost all the way
through and another boy did the same with his. You
pointed them at each other, touched both at once with
your slow matches, and they fizzed and spat at each other
in a cat and dog fight.

After a while it was time for the parade. A parade with beautiful horses prancing along as the band played "Yankee Doodle." Some of the men who rode — the young ones — were soldiers. Others — the old ones — were men who had marched to Lexington in 1775. They wore their old cocked hats and some of them still wore powder in their hair. Marching in the hot dust were the Masons from the Boston Lodge wearing their embroidered aprons and their big jeweled badges with the amethysts and the golden squares and compasses. Marching too were groups of sturdy red-cheeked truckmen in their white frocks. It was hot work marching and when the parade was over, the marchers would picnic in the shade of the big twisty-armed white oak at the end of Harrison Place.

Harrison Place was just a country lane then. An old cart path ran out of it and down to the big oak and past it toward the salt marsh where the hay would soon be cut. At low tide the Muddy River made a wide brown pathway through the marsh. At high tide the water gleamed and shone through it and the whole marsh seemed to be floating. Wild ducks swam in the bright pools and sea gulls, with the tips of their wings looking as if they had been dipped in ink, sailed in over the marsh, crying like lost cats as they swooped down for fish.

There was a clear, cold spring under the oak and there the picnic was spread and the punch was made. Boys used to like to suck the leftover lemon rinds. Sometimes there would be more than a bushel . . .

"What would the girls be doing all this time?" Susie asked.

The girls — her grandmother told her — were either at home learning to be young ladies or out in public practicing what they had learned. On Fourth of July they would probably be watching the parade, dressed of course in their best embroidered muslins. They would definitely not be under the white oak sucking lemon rinds. On other days, when they had finished their stints of sewing or spinning, they were sometimes allowed to go for a "ramble" and pick wild flowers. Mrs. Goddard wrote about one of her young visitors who went for a ramble and got into some poison ivy with unhappy results. That seemed to be the high spot of the visit.

The girls' stints corresponded to the boys' chores — keeping the wood box filled, helping around the barn, driving the cows to pasture. The only trouble from the point of view of a girl was that her tasks kept her sitting in the house while the boy's took him out into the fields. When a girl's stint of weaving or spinning or mending was done, she was allowed to work on her sampler. She would draw the pattern herself, copying from other samplers. She might draw a house at the top and a border of flowers as big as the house with birds sitting among them, strange birds bigger than the flowers. Then she would do rows of letters of the alphabet and numbers and some piece of good advice to the young. The kind of advice that might possibly be taken by the old — if by anyone — and would say something like this:

See the little day star moving.
Life and time are worth improving.
Seize the moment while you may;
Seize and use it, lest you lose it
And lament the wasted day.

Underneath would be the name and age of the maker. The one who worked this one with the yellow house — I found it in the trunk — was twelve years old. Every stitch had to be perfectly done or it had to be taken out. Of course she couldn't start as soon as she had made the design. She would have to begin by weaving the linen and dyeing the embroidery thread.

"Didn't they do anything else?" Susie asked with a slight groan.

"Yes — they netted purses and covered them with beads like this one that came out of the trunk. They made hair bracelets and wreaths of dried flowers and seeds. They baked bread, dipped candles, embroidered caps and collars . . ."

"Didn't they study anything? Didn't they have any fun on Sundays?"

On Sundays — her grandmother said — they couldn't even work on their samplers! Sunday began on Saturday night at sundown and lasted until sun set on Sunday. They went to meeting. Twice usually. They did the necessary work around the house — made the beds, got the meals. Most of the cooking for Sunday was done on Saturday.

I liked to have my grandmother tell me what I used to

call the story of The Jinitin Tree. It shows what Sunday was like in the eighteen-twenties. Children had very few books then but on Sundays they were not allowed to read even the few they had — *Ivanhoe,* or *The Talisman,* for instance. They could read sermons or the Bible. They couldn't play any games. They could listen to the conversation of the grownups but the talk was either intended for the improvement of the young or had to do with sickness or death.

The worst Sundays of the whole year, my grandmother told me, were the ones in June when the sun set later and later and they had longer and longer to wait until the Sabbath was over. Of course they had extra long to play the evening before but naturally no child thinks of that twenty-four hours later. One thing that made waiting especially hard was that they were all hungry for fruit.

They longed especially for apples. And the apples from the last season were gone long before June. There was rhubarb but no one ever seemed to put enough sugar in it. There were wild strawberries, but who ever picked enough for a family of ten people including several hungry boys? Still, there was something wonderful in their orchard, the only one they had ever heard of — an apple tree that bore its fruit in June. June Eating Apples, their father called the juicy, sweet yellow globes. The children, however, had talked about the apples so often and so fast that June Eating became Jinitin and they called it the Jinitin Tree.

They watched it from the time in the early spring when its little scarlet knobs opened into pink and white flowers with bees buzzing in and out of them. They saw the petals blow away in white drifts and shrivel and turn brown. They found the first hard green buttons and waited for them to grow bigger, to turn yellow on the sunny side, to be delicately striped with pink. Somehow, my grandmother said — though probably it was not really so — it always seemed to be Sunday when they were fully ripe and on Sunday the children were not allowed to go near the tree. Even if an apple, heavier than the rest, fell into the grass with a soft thud, they could not pick up the fallen fruit.

They could not even look at it most of the day because they were in church so long, three hours in the morning and three more in the afternoon. At last they all sat in a row on the doorstep — all seven of them, four boys, three girls — waiting for the sun to go down. As it crawled through the sky, it shone through the Jinitin Tree. They sat, elbows on knees, chins on hands, staring at the tree. The apples were gold, then they were dark, edged with gold, then they and the twigs, leaves, and twisted branches were black against the huge copper disk. At last the trunk stood out against the blazing light. Now the sun was going down faster and faster. Its rim dipped behind the hill, it burned red. With one last flash it was gone.

"And then," said Susie, "how they must have raced for the tree!"

No — said her grandmother — not yet. They walked to their rooms, took off their Sabbath Day clothes, folded them neatly, and dressed in their ordinary clothes. The boys waited honorably for the girls. Petticoats took longer to change than pantaloons. But at last — at last they were ready. Even Sophronia, my grandmother, the youngest of all, was ready and was given a head start.

Then David's voice rang out: "Race you, race you — one, two, three. Hey ho, hey ho for the Jinitin Tree!"

"Well," said Andrew, "I hope the apples were good!"

"According to my grandmother no apples ever tasted like them and I can well believe it."

"So even the girls raced?" said Susie.

"Yes, even the girls — and they played tag around the rosebushes afterwards. Life wasn't all Sundays. They had fun on other days, playing games, going to singing school and to dances."

Susie asked what they danced.

"Lady Walpole's Reel, quadrilles, Hull's Victory," her grandmother said.

"You mean Balance Four in Line — the way we dance?" Andrew asked.

"Yes, the very same calls. The dance was made up to celebrate Captain Isaac Hull's victory over the British in the War of 1812. It was one of the earliest American dances and a popular dance all over New England."

The tune is the same too — she went on. The difference is in the clothes people wore. High, stiff collars, ruffled shirts, blue coats with brass buttons for the men. Low-necked, high-waisted dresses of silk or muslin with narrow skirts for the girls. They dressed much the same way for singing school and some of the happiest evenings were spent there. All ages joined in. They sang the

familiar hymns that were sung in the meetinghouse on
Sundays, songs about the Revolution, songs full of words
that were hard to say. The singing master made them get
every syllable perfectly clear while they sang:

The turkey's in the pan and the dowdy's at the fire
And we're all getting ready for Cousin Jedediah, for Cousin
*   Jedediah*
And Zachariah and Hezekiah and Aunt Sophia . . .

Girls often had private music lessons too — she added.
When a girl went out in the evening her hostess would ask
her to sing or play something, in case she had her music
with her and the guest would reply shyly: "I must see if
I have anything . . . I think I just happened to slip a few
sheets in my muff."

Mrs. Goddard wrote to Mehitable that her niece Louisa
had been to a musical evening in Boston but that Louisa
didn't care for the "fashionable singing" of some of the
performers. Fashionable or homemade, there was plenty
of music in Brookline all through the nineteenth century.
Energetic young ladies thumped out duets on the piano.
People met at each others' houses and played trios and
quartets. There was a Trio Club that used to meet even
when I was a little girl and I have gone to sleep plenty
of times with the sound of Mozart or Beethoven in my
ears. Sometimes a hostess would engage a fiddler and a
harpist. Brown Holland linen would be tacked down all
over the carpet and soon everyone would be dancing.
Young Dr. Wild rushed around so fast and swung his
partners so violently that he was considered a menace to

life and limb, but everyone liked him and no party was complete without him.

"Perhaps school was fun too," Susie suggested, hopefully. "You haven't told us anything about that yet."

If you went to school in Brookline at the brick schoolhouse any time after 1816 — her grandmother said — you would have gone to school to Master Isaac Adams. This early Brookline schoolhouse was built on the triangle near the meetinghouse in 1793. It was a square, hip-roofed building without blinds, porch, or shed. There were both boys and girls in the school — thirty or forty altogether. Their ages ran from four to eighteen. No child who went to school to Master Adams seemed to remember much about what he studied in the brick schoolhouse, but no one ever forgot Master Adams.

He began the day with a long prayer, during which his eyes and ears were open for the slightest noise or movement. After the prayer, the punishments of the day began. Perhaps no one had done anything wrong but Master Adams acted on the theory that a whipping is never wasted on a boy because if he has not just done a piece of mischief, he is just going to.

His chief weapon was called a clapper. This was a circular piece of leather about three quarters of an inch thick and six inches across. It had a hole in the middle and looked rather like a large tough doughnut. It was fastened to a strong, limber leather handle about two feet long. Master Adams kept this instrument of education not in the school, but at his lodging. The first offender of the morning was sent for it. The thoughts of the spanking that was to come must have made the walk a gloomy one. Still, he must hurry to his doom. The longer the errand took, the longer and harder the clapper would be at work.

Perhaps while he was gone some other luckless scholar might whisper or giggle. The master would then send out for a sapling (the woods were near) about four feet long. With his knife he would trim off part of the leaves and split the thick end enough so that the criminal's nose could be inserted in the crack. Thus decorated, the giggler would stand before the school. Girls sometimes had their ears thrust into the cleft stick. At other times they were merely made to sit on the unipod, as Master Adams called a stool he had invented. It had one leg in the middle and to stay right side up on it for any length of time took almost as good a sense of balance as is needed for riding a bicycle. Naturally if the rider fell down, more punishments were to be expected. Master Adams could always think of something.

It was not only the older children who were supposed to practice perfect behavior. Even the four- and five-year-olds who sat in a row on a long low seat in the front of the room were punished if they did anything besides sit up straight and keep still.

Of course bright healthy children cannot possibly sit quiet hour after hour when the only thing they are called on to do all day is to recite the letters from A to Z. Of course, also, Master Adams had no patience with children who squirmed or wriggled or swung their feet. One day, long remembered, the infant class was so trying to his sense of order that he seized one of the four-year-old sinners and laid him face down on the platform where the teacher's desk stood. Others were laid beside him, others above until a pyramid was formed with the chief offender on top. Then, seizing the clapper, the master applied it vigorously to the topmost pupil while groans and cries in every key came from the struggling heap.

Miss Harriet Woods, who tells this story in a book about Brookline written in 1874, remarks that "had there been less elasticity in these little martyrs, our town might have been minus its present worthy treasurer as well as sundry other good citizens."

On another occasion a little four-year-old boy, who walked a mile to school every day with his older sister, fell asleep one hot midsummer afternoon. Naturally this was a serious crime and he must be punished. The master stepped lightly over to the small sleeper, with his handkerchief deftly tied the boy's feet to a large umbrella, and gave this to a big boy in the row behind with orders to hold it firmly.

Then, going back to his place, he stamped on the floor, shouting, "Daniel! Come here!"

The poor child jumped up out of his sleep and of course fell down and began to cry. His sister cried too and was jeered at by the master and punished before the school for her weakness.

"You sound awfully mad, Grandma," Andrew said.

"Probably," his grandmother said, "because I am. I don't like tyranny and injustice to defenseless people wherever or whenever they happened."

It seems hard to believe — she went on — that at the time when Master Adams was torturing small children, no one objected. Indeed a child who was punished in school was often punished again at home. Master Adams was not told to take his ideas of education somewhere else. Far from it. He taught in Brookline for almost twenty years. To say that he was remembered by his scholars is to put it mildly.

Better days were on the way. School came to be taught by men and women who were firm with their pupils but who liked them and understood them. One of the chief excitements of school all through the nineteenth century was the spelling match. It was so when Sophronia raced for the Jinitin Tree, when her daughter, Mary Edgerly, was learning Latin from her brother at the age of six, and when I used to go to the Lawrence School years later.

A gift for spelling is something like an ear for music, or red hair and freckles — they all come naturally. Sophronia was one of those natural spellers. If one of her big brothers was captain of the spelling team, he always began by choosing Sophronia, one of the smallest children in the school, and she "spelled down" many older and larger spellers.

The way of spelling a word was first to pronounce it clearly and then to take it to pieces, pronouncing and spelling it out syllable by syllable, adding a new syllable to the pronunciation each time. Until you had finally pronounced the whole word at the end, you could change your mind and go back to the beginning. After you had once said the completed word, if you had made a mistake, you were sent back to your seat.

The letters written at this time are often modeled on books that gave examples of letters for every occasion. You could find out how to thank your godfather for a silver teaspoon or how to express sympathy for your aunt on the loss of her pet Maltese cat.

"Are you making this up by any chance?" Susie asked.

"Well, yes," her grandmother admitted. "But you would be surprised if you read some of the old Compleat Letter Writers and etiquette books to see how many situations they covered."

"Such as?" Susie suggested.

"Sophronia's etiquette book might give you some idea. Here it is. It's been read almost to pieces, you see."

"Who wrote it?" Susie asked.

Her grandmother said that the author on the title page just called himself a gentleman and that he gave a great deal of useful advice. If a man went out to dinner in those days, he would find that the dining table was covered with two tablecloths, one on top of the other. When he first sat down, there might be on the table a roast goose, a pigeon pie, a ham, dishes of vegetables, apple sauce, pickles, and a dish of turbot with lobster sauce. After the first course was over, all the dishes and plates and silver, and the upper tablecloth itself were taken away. Pies, cakes, puddings, and custards were then put on the table. After they had been eaten, the second cloth was taken away and the dessert — nuts, raisins, and wine — would be placed on the bare, polished mahogany. The men were expected to carve or serve whatever was placed in front of them. Some men were better carvers than others. Here is a letter from a young man who had an embarrassing experience at such a dinner. He is consulting the author about what to do in such circumstances.

It seems that when he sat down at the table, he was asked to carve a roast goose that was just in front of him. He had never carved one before and a goose is especially hard to carve. The joints always seem to come where no sensible bird would have joints. The young carver had trouble from the first. The goose was not only tough, it was slippery and before many minutes of the battle had gone on, it skidded off the platter, slid across the corner of the table, and landed in the gray satin lap of a lady with a turban and a stern expression.

"What should a gentleman do in a case like that?" asked the young man desperately.

The author, like most authors, was delighted to tell him.

"If such an awkward situation occurs again," he wrote, "simply look the lady straight in the eye and say, 'Madam, I'll trouble you for that goose.'"

"Do you suppose he did?" Susie asked.

"I suppose," said her grandmother, "that from then on he was careful to sit near the mashed potatoes."

Being a good carver — she went on — was part of a man's work because there were such big families and so many people sat down at the table together.

"I can remember Grandpapa carving," Susie said. "He

always made the knife very sharp first. It shone and I liked the noise."

Yes, he carved beautifully. No geese ever skidded into anyone's lap. He didn't have to shop for the goose first though. But back in the early nineteenth century the men of the family often did the marketing. They would take their own big market baskets in their own carriages to Faneuil Hall Market, fill them with good things and have their coachmen drive them home — to their Boston houses in the winter, to Brookline in the summer. You could see whatever there was in the basket because there were no paper bags. If you bought anything that had to be wrapped up — butter or cheese, for instance — it would be wrapped in a page torn from an old book, perhaps a book of sermons or a page from some old manuscript. Paper in those days was expensive. It was made of linen rags and you didn't just throw it away. A great many things that we'd like to read now were said to have "gone to the butter makers" or "gone to the trunk makers." Pages from some of the most important books ever written by a resident of Brookline may have been used to line trunks or hatboxes or to wrap up chocolate.

The author, well-known in Brookline, whose books are rare today, was Miss Hannah Adams. She was the exception to the rule that girls were fit only to do household tasks and in their spare time paint on velvet. She was a girl during the Revolution, a time when it was almost unheard of for a woman to study Latin and Greek, but Miss Adams learned both. She had very little money and she tried to support herself in the few ways that a woman at that time could earn a living. She made lace. She braided straw for bonnets. She taught school.

"Was she related to Master Adams?" Andrew asked.

"Not so far as I know," his grandmother said. "Certainly she was a very different kind of person. She found teaching hard on her nerves. When Master Adams taught, it was the pupils' nerves that suffered."

Miss Adams — she went on — gave up teaching and turned to writing. At that time there was no history of this part of the country that even mentioned the Revolutionary War. Miss Adams went back over old documents and wrote a history of New England that was widely read for many years and on which many later books are based. She also wrote books in which she used her knowledge of Greek and Latin. This was such an unusual thing that people gazed upon the author as if she were some sort of human curiosity. She was, in fact, a little different from other people. She was so much interested in something that might have happened two thousand years ago that she often did not notice what was going on around her.

Once she stayed all night in the house of a friend and slept for the first time in a room where the door had a knob instead of a latch. When she tried to get out in the morning, she found that this strange-looking round thing on the door would not lift up or pull out or go down. It never occurred to her to turn it, so she sat down patiently and sank happily back into ancient Rome until someone came and let her out.

Traveling was hard for her because she knew she might

forget something. Once on a stagecoach a man, who had heard that she talked interestingly on many subjects, tried to start a conversation with her. All he heard her say, as the coach bounced and rattled along, was: "Great trunk, little trunk, bandbox, and bundle. Great trunk, little trunk . . ." until the journey was over. If in her moments of silence Miss Adams had any interesting thoughts about Marcus Aurelius or Edmund Burke or King Solomon, no one heard them. Once when she was staying at the house of a Mr. Perkins in Leverett Street in Boston, she got into a hackney coach and absent-mindedly told the driver to take her to Mr. Leverett's in Perkins Street. The man drove around the city until eleven o'clock at night trying to find Perkins Street. Miss Adams took no interest in his problem but relaxed happily with her own thoughts. At last the driver went back to the livery stable and desperately asked the owner of the hack what to do.

The stablekeeper came out and looked into the carriage.

"Oh," he said, "that's Miss Hannah Adams! Take her to Mr. Perkins's in Leverett Street."

We know how she looked because there is a portrait of her in the Boston Athenaeum. She is wearing a simple Quakerish-looking gray dress, a lawn kerchief, and a close white cap — possibly the very one she carried in the bandbox that she worried about on that journey.

Miss Adams died in Brookline in 1832 when she was seventy-five years old. She loved the sunshine and the green fields and hills of the country town where she spent her last days. To one of her visitors she showed the view from her window and said: "How can anyone be tired of such a beautiful world?"

Even people far away from Brookline still remembered those green hills and dreamed of seeing them again. All those years that Mehitable and Samuel Goddard lived in England they must both have thought of coming home again and have wondered where they would live. At last the day came when they sailed into Boston Harbor, saw the State House, the church spires they knew — Old North, Old South, Park Street — walked again on the Common past the Old Elm, looked out across the waters of the Back Bay and saw the Brookline hills.

They stayed in Boston for a time but Samuel Goddard did not think his family ought to spend the summer there. One morning he called on a friend of his, a Mr. Howe, and asked if his friend knew of a house near the sea where his wife and children could have fresh air and sunshine. Mr. Howe said that he could not think of one that Mr. Goddard would like.

"But," he said, "I can tell you about something that might interest you. Do you remember the old Babcock place in Brookline?"

Of course Samuel Goddard remembered the old Babcock place, the flowers, the smooth lawns, the high white columns, the wallpaper where the river ran past Constantinople. He could almost see himself, still a small redheaded boy, leaning over the fence, almost taste the gingerbread that appeared when Madam Babcock knocked with her stick on the wall.

"It's to be sold at auction this afternoon," Mr. Howe went on. "I thought I would go out —— not to buy it, you know — just to see how it goes. The sale starts in an hour but we have time. My chaise is at the door. Will you drive with me? Shall we go?"

They were just in time, driving along the Mill Dam, past the Punch Bowl, up Walnut Street, through sunshine and green shade. The little boy who used to look at the house and think, It's the most beautiful house in the world . . . If I were only a man . . . If I were only rich . . . bought the house that afternoon and lived in it happily for the rest of his life — And Mehitable was back again in her much loved Brookline.

IF, IN THE YEAR 1800, you were to ask an old-time resident of Brookline, an old soldier who still wore a camlet cloak and a cocked hat and knee breeches, when some old house or other was built, he would probably reply, "Well, I know it was there before the Revolution. We marched right past it when we went to Lexington."

That was the way things were dated by everyone. Everything that happened before the first shot was fired on Lexington Green was before the Revolution. Even Mehitable Goddard's father, William Dawes, rode through the village past the Punch Bowl before the Revolution. The next day was the beginning of freedom from Great Britain. The alarm spread rapidly through Brookline. Guns were already cleaned. Now they were taken down from above the big fireplaces. Powder horns were already filled and there were plenty of bullets in the leather bullet bags. Small boys had been molding bullets for

weeks, melting up pewter platters and plates and teapots
and pouring the hot metal into bullet molds. It was no
surprise to anyone in Brookline to hear that the British
were going to march out to Concord — where the colony
kept its military stores. Everyone knew that sometime the
British would try to destroy the cannon and powder and
shot at Concord. What William Dawes, riding out along
Boston Neck, crossing the Muddy River, hearing the sign
of the Punch Bowl creak as it swung on its red post, was
telling was: "The British are coming — tomorrow."

In Brookline, as in other New England towns, the men
were ready. They needed only to know the day and the
hour. For the past three years Brookline had had a Committee of Correspondence. It was appointed to consult
with other towns and to assert the rights of the colony
against Great Britain. Since January 1, 1775, Brookline
had had a volunteer company of soldiers. So on that
beautiful warm April morning — spring was early that
year and the leaves on the elms were already bigger than
a squirrel's ears — every able-bodied man of Brookline
met on the green triangle at the center of the town where
Walnut and Warren Streets run together. Every man,
that is, but one. There was one who did not appear. He
explained afterwards that he just couldn't seem to get
ready in time. His neighbors accepted the explanation.
They knew he was not a Tory — that he was just moderate, as we say in Vermont. They did not mention his
name when they wrote about the battle.

The names of the men who met on the Green had been
known since the early days of the town — Aspinwall,

Griggs, Crafts, Gardner, Winchester. Dr William Aspinwall started for the battle wearing his best scarlet coat,
but a friend told him that he might be mistaken for a
British "red coat" so the doctor changed to a coat of a
quieter color. He was a big man, over six feet tall, and
is said to have looked so much like Washington that in
New York a group of rioters once spared a portrait of
Dr. Aspinwall because they mistook it for a picture of the
General. When Dr. Aspinwall was a small boy, he was
hit in the right eye by an arrow. He lost the sight of that
eye but he was nevertheless a fine shot, although he had
to fire his gun from his left shoulder. More than one
bullet he fired that day met its mark.

Dr. Aspinwall ended his fighting with the Battle of
Lexington, joined the Medical Corps of the Army, and
served with distinction in it. He said he would rather
save Americans than kill Britishers. His services ended
only with the end of the war.

Another Brookline doctor who took part in the Battle
of Lexington was Dr. Downer. He lived in the Punch
Bowl Village in a house beautifuly shaded by elms and
buttonwoods. Although he was considered an excellent
surgeon, he was a harsh rough man. Perhaps before the
invention of ether when the patients were conscious
during operations, a certain amount of harshness was
necessary. At least Dr. Downer showed his courage when,
on his way home from the battle, he met a British soldier
and fought him hand to hand, at last running him through
with his bayonet.

The captain of the militia company was Isaac Gardner,

a much loved citizen of the town. His family was large —
he had eight children. One September night, seven years
before the Revolution, his house and all his furniture
were destroyed by fire. The fire happened on a Friday
and it made eighteen people homeless. Brookline was a
small country town then. There were only fifty families
and they were struggling under the burden of British
taxation. Yet by Monday the neighbors had raised a
hundred pounds to help the Gardners rebuild their house.

"People were very nice to us in California when our
house burned down," Susie said.

Her grandmother said that she thought that kindness
and neighborliness were about the best things a town
could have and that luckily they didn't go out of fashion.

The sad thing for the town as well as for Captain
Gardner's family — she went on — was that he was killed
in the Battle of Lexington. When the American troops
were on their way back from Lexington he stopped in
Cambridge to drink from a well and was hit by six British
bullets.

Dr. Aspinwall took care of his friend's body and it was
brought back to Brookline the next day in a wagon by
another friend and neighbor, John Heath. The whole
town, as well as his own family, grieved for Mr. Gardner.
His death was the worst blow the town received in the
battle.

British troops, twelve hundred of them in their scarlet coats, marched through Brookline on their way to
Lexington but did no damage to property. In fact the
town was never involved in any fighting, although it was

close enough to the enemy to have a fort. This Brookline
Fort was near where the Muddy River runs into the
Charles River. Brookline actually had a seacoast at that
time. The Charles and the Muddy River were both tidal
rivers and the salty tides of the Atlantic washed up them.
You could reach Pond Avenue in Brookline by boat.
Later the part of Brookline that fronted on the Charles
became part of Boston but in the Revolution the fort was
in Brookline. It was commanded by another member
of the Aspinwall family — Colonel Thomas Aspinwall.
It had six cannon. Near St. Mary's Street, there was also
a battery of two guns.

Naturally there was great excitement in Brookline
when the news came that General Washington himself
was coming to inspect the fort. Every boy in town wanted
to see the General and most of them did.

Some of the men who ran across lots through Brookline
and Newton to be sure to get to Lexington in time for
the battle had long years of fighting before they left the
army. One of them was a man named Jacob Harvey,
who enlisted in the Continental Army for three years.
He was paid "the sum of fifty hard dollars and three
thousand seven hundred and fifty Continental dollars" a
year. It was also agreed that his wife was to have four
cords of good firewood delivered to her house each year.
His wife, like many women of the time, had never learned
to read and write and she signed a receipt for the money
by making a cross opposite her name, which was written
by someone else — like this: Mary Harvey X Her mark.

The sums of money paid to Jacob Harvey for his serv-

ices show one of the great hardships of the war — the
troubles the colonies had with their money affairs. The
fifty dollars in "hard money" — that is, in silver, gold, or
even copper — was something that anyone would accept
in any business transaction. The $3750 in Continental
dollars was supposed to be worth the same as the fifty
dollars in hard money. At least at the time Jacob Harvey
enlisted a hard dollar was worth 75 Continental dollars
but it was often difficult to get anything in return for a
Continental dollar.

"Is that what someone meant last summer when he
said the hay crop wasn't worth a Continental?" Andrew
asked.

"I suppose so," his grandmother said. "A Continental
certainly wasn't worth much."

People sometimes took advantage of this situation —
she went on. The minister's salary — three hundred
dollars perhaps — had been promised on the basis of hard
money. Some towns paid their ministers in Continental
dollars. Brookline however dealt honorably with the
minister of the time, Mr. Jackson. Town and church
were the same thing at the time of the Revolution. To
be a citizen of the town you must be a member of the
church and the expenses of the church were paid for out
of the town taxes. In spite of the fact that money was
scarce for everyone, the people of Brookline paid Mr.
Jackson enough more than the salary he had been promised to make up all his living expenses.

Mr. Jackson was a man much respected by the older
members of the church, but to the children of the town

his old-fashioned clothes, powdered wig, and stern appearance were frightening.

Miss Woods tells a story that shows how the boys of the town felt. At that time families did not sit together in the meetinghouse. Men sat on one side of the church, women on the other, and the children all sat in the gallery. All around the gallery ran a long low balustrade. One Sunday a stray dog trotted into the church, walked up the gallery steps, jumped up on top of the balustrade, and calmly walked along it, apparently looking with interest at the minister, in his high pulpit under the sounding board that was like a huge cap above his head, and at the rest of the congregation.

Naturally the dog was a good deal more interesting to the boys than a long sermon full of hard words. It is not quite clear how what followed happened. Perhaps the boys were trying to get hold of the dog. Perhaps he slipped on the polished wood. Anyway he landed suddenly in the pew below and in spite of the minister's stern frown and the tything man's stick, the boys giggled like — well, like boys.

The next day the dignified minister was seen walking up the hill toward the meetinghouse. It was recess time at the old schoolhouse and the boys were playing games — leap frog, or White Men and Indians, or kicking the football. By the time Mr. Jackson arrived at the schoolhouse, there was not a boy in sight. Behind fences or trees, behind the great piece of pudding stone where the Wishing Stone is, cautiously edging around behind the meetinghouse, they had scattered like a covey of par-

tridges in the autumn woods. They were as invisible to
the minister as young partridges or as Indians lurking in
a dark forest.

Even the girls of the parish, model little girls who sat
on cushions and sewed fine seams every day and who
copied poetry off tombstones for their samplers, were
afraid of Mr. Jackson. When he called at a house, the
children used to disappear until the visit was over. Many
of them would hide behind a stone wall when they saw
him coming rather than meet him and have to make the
bow or curtsy to him that were the custom of the times.

Mr. Jackson had one human weakness. He smoked
and he had a tin case for his long clay pipes and a pair of
tongs so that he could take a hot coal from the fire and
light a pipe with it. Matches had not been invented, so
fires were lighted either by borrowing some coals from a
neighbor or by using flint and steel to strike a spark, and
a tinderbox.

"What is tinder?" Andrew asked.

"Something that was very dry and would light easily
and keep the spark alive until you had enough flame to
start a fire. Scorched linen was one thing that was used
for tinder," his grandmother said.

When the girls of the family had some spare time —
she went on — they rolled pieces of paper into long narrow spills, as they were called. If you wanted to light a
candle, you would first light a spill at the fireplace and
then transfer the flame to the candlewick. If you were
lighting a good many candles, a spill might be more convenient than a match because it burned longer.

"Did they have matches when you were a little girl?" Susie asked.

"Yes, but not like the ones they have now," her grandmother said.

She went on to tell them that old-fashioned matches were not scratched on the box. They were called sulphur matches and they were made of wood and tipped with a reddish orange substance. They came in cards, more than a dozen to a card, and were scratched on a piece of sandpaper. Children used to make match scratchers for their grandmothers for Christmas. A favorite pattern showed a kitten and a cat and said: Don't scratch me, scratch Mother! The cat's back was made of sandpaper.

Sulphur matches made a delicious fiery smell when they were scratched. There was also another kind of match called a wax vesta. These were like little candles and as they were imported from England, they were rather expensive. Most people used the sulphur kind. There were still some old-fashioned people who thought that any match at all was an extravagant luxury, and dangerous too. They kept glasses of spills on the mantelpiece.

"I suppose in the Revolution when they didn't have matches, people spent a lot of time in the firelight," Susie said.

Her grandmother said that she supposed most Brookline people at that time, like farmers everywhere, got up with the sun and went to bed with it for a good part of the year. The men plowed and planted and harvested their grains and vegetables. They cut wood and sawed and split it. They made hay and put it into barns that they had built with their own hands. There were always animals to take care of. When they had any spare time, they tinkered at odd jobs — carpentry, bricklaying, harness making, painting. They would set a pane of glass or make pump logs and lay them so that water would run right from the spring to a barrel in the yard. They laid stone walls and planted fruit trees. Sooner or later a man usually held some town office. He might be chosen fence viewer, constable, sealer of leather, weigher of bread, town clerk, selectman, or even the town's representative to the General Court of the Commonwealth.

The women were just as busy — spinning, dyeing, weaving, knitting stockings, making clothes for themselves and their children, or making their husbands' shirts and washing them, and making the soap to wash them with. They baked their own bread, corned their own beef, took care of hens and turkeys and made dusters of the turkey feathers. They dried apples and herbs. They made corn into hominy and made mattresses of the husks. From the straw beehives under the apple trees, they got honey to eat with corn bread. The bees also supplied them with wax to polish the highboy and the tea table. They made twenty-pound cheeses that had to be turned every day for months.

If new spoons were needed, they made them at home out of pewter. Usually this was something the boys did.

"How?" asked Andrew.

"About the same way they made bullets," his grandmother said. "There usually were some damaged pieces of pewter around the house. They melted them and

poured the hot metal into a mold. I have a mold. Your
Uncle Sam made some for me once. I'll have to let you
use it sometime."

"And I suppose," said Susie gloomily, "that the girls
as usual were just making those samplers."

"Not just samplers," her grandmother said. "They
also embroidered pictures."

Susie groaned slightly and asked what the pictures were
like.

Nothing that will make you feel any more cheerful — her grandmother told her. A favorite subject was
a path leading to a church. Near it, under a bright green
weeping willow, was a white monument with an urn on
top. Two dreary-looking females in trailing black robes
stood beside the monument. Like the willows, they were
weeping. In families where deaths had occurred, there
were names and dates on the monument. In cases of
happier families the monuments were left blank but the
black-robed ladies wept anyway, in advance.

"Where did they learn to embroider?" Susie asked.

"In school," her grandmother said. "There were always small private schools where such accomplishments
were taught. These schools sprang up, lasted a few years,
and then disappeared. Edward Atkinson used to go to
school, much later of course, in the same building where
girls used to learn embroidery. Later still it became a
hen house. He went in to look at the old building one
day. His desk was still there. A hen flew right out of it."

Don't think — she added — that the children didn't
have any fun. Many of them went to school in an old

schoolhouse near where the Pierce School now is. It stood
on what was called School House Lane and was the only
building on it until 1830. The lane was very narrow.
An oxcart could just pass between the low stone walls that
bordered it. Trees grew thickly beyond the walls and in
one place the wall was nearly hidden by barberry bushes.
When their tiny yellow blossoms opened the lane had a
heavy honey sweet smell.

Under the barberry bushes the girls used to play house
with bits of broken china or glass for dishes. They made
seats of pieces of board and covered them with scraps of
old quilts. They built fireplaces and chimneys of stones.
They made beds of straw, covered their wooden dolls with
scraps of old coverlets, and put them to sleep. The
wooden dolls were far from beautiful, if this one from
the old trunk is any sample. Yet children played with her
for more than a hundred years. Her name was Wooden
Mary. You couldn't break her and even when she was
left out in the rain and snow for most of a winter, her
honest countenance merely weathered slightly.

Girls could do certain things better than boys. One
thing girls were good at was rolling hoops. Another was
skipping rope while someone called, "Salt, vinegar, mustard, pepper!" In winter both boys and girls constructed
coasts, piling up snow for jounces in the tracks. They all
hung on hard at the bumps and tried to see who could
yell the loudest. They had snowball fights. The boys
threw the snowballs, of course, but the girls were allowed
to make them. They helped make snow men too, with
pieces of charcoal for eyes. They slid on frozen ponds.

There were hidden ponds in the swamps if you knew how to find them.

When spring came and the snow melted, the boys built rafts and poled them through the salty marshes. In summer they fished and swam in the brooks. They rode horses and helped in the haymaking. Girls sometimes helped make hay too. There were hay rides in September when the moon was full. When the frosts came again in October both boys and girls went into the woods and hunted for chestnuts.

"Horse chestnuts?" Andrew asked.

"No, real chestnuts, a kind that doesn't grow now. The trees all died of a blight in the early years of this century," his grandmother told him.

Children went to school in a building on the lane even while Brookline was still part of Boston — she said. Girls went to school more than boys because boys who were big enough to help on the farm had most of their schooling in the winter when there was the least farm work to do. A man usually taught the winter term and a school mistress the other terms. A man was needed to keep the older boys in order at a time when the methods of keeping peace in the schoolroom included throwing a knife or a mahogany ruler across the room and administering beatings with a cane. Master Adams was not the only schoolmaster who beat his scholars.

The school building consisted of one room, not a large one, with a sort of alley running down the middle of it. Facing this alley on both sides were long narrow benches made of heavy planks. In front of these were other planks

on legs. These were the desks. They had drawers underneath in which books — the Bible, Psalter, Arithmetic,
and Spelling Book — could be kept. The teacher's desk
was in the left-hand corner away from the door. There
were pegs on which clothes were hung along the walls.
In the right hand corner there was an enormous chimney
with a great cavern of a fireplace.

The wood for this fireplace was piled outside, un-
covered. Rain and snow fell freely upon it and as it was
often green to start with, it cannot have been very easy
to burn. The master's school began the Monday after
Thanksgiving so fires were needed all through the term.
The boys of the school took turns sawing and splitting the
wood and making the fires. Since there were no matches
and it took a long time to get a fire going with flint and
steel and tinder, the boy's first task was to go every
morning to the nearest house — Squire Sharp's — carrying an iron skillet. This he filled with live coals from the
Squire's fireplace and brought them back to the schoolhouse to light the chips and shavings used for kindling.
On a cold morning one of the boys, after working with
his axe on a green and knotty stump without making
much impression, had the bright idea of blowing it up
with gunpowder. He drilled a hole, filled it with powder,
made a trail of powder running from the hole, touched
the end of the trail with a hot coal, and waited to see what
happened. When he hit the ground again, he had learned
something about explosives. He was lame for some time
afterwards.

Fires made of this green wood often smoked. One

morning there was such a thick smoke that the room was
completely filled with it. Even when doors and windows
were opened, the air was so smoky that lessons were impossible so the choking, coughing pupils were dismissed.
When the fire was out and the chimney inspected, it was
found that its top was completely and carefully covered
with a board. Just who it was who provided the holiday
was never known.

Perhaps it did no harm to have an occasional holiday.
Even the four-year-olds sat on those hard benches from
nine to twelve in the morning and from one to four in the
afternoon in the icy days of winter and the broiling ones
of summer. There was a five-minute recess in the morning and another in the afternoon. To keep any sort of
order in the schoolroom, even the women teachers did a
great deal of shaking and slapping and striking of open
palms with the ruler. For these services they were paid
at most two dollars and a half a week. Whether the
children learned anything was unimportant compared to
how still they sat. The idea was that while children might
not look exactly like lions or tigers, they were really only
a slightly different type of wild animal and that the way
to keep them from eating the teacher alive was to have a
whip always on view. It is not very strange that many
children finished their schooling without even being able
to read and write well or to spell or figure accurately.

"Anyone who can't read and write must be pretty
dumb," Andrew said.

Not necessarily — his grandmother said. Reading and
writing are useful tools but they don't make people

intelligent of themselves. We have a prejudice in favor of them. At the time of the Revolution there were plenty of people who had a prejudice against them. They were often regarded as a kind of magic by which shrewd and dishonest people took advantage of simple and honest ones. A man who had no book learning was often intelligent in other ways.

Once some children who were digging near the schoolhouse — the one in School House Lane — at recess time, found a cannon ball buried in the mud. They liked to think that it had been fired from a British cannon but there is no record that the British ever fired a shot in Brookline. Probably it was an American cannon ball. Perhaps it fell from John Goddard's wagon some dark night while this citizen of Brookline was helping to prepare for the Siege of Boston.

From July, 1775, until the following March, the town of Boston was encircled by Washington's troops. Inside the town were the British forces commanded by General Howe. The Tory families who sympathized with the British and who expected that the impudent rebels would soon be put in their places, were there too. Those who opposed British rule had left — if they could. The men joined the Continental Army. Their wives and children went to stay with relatives and friends who lived farther inland.

Of course there were many who could not leave and they must have watched the ring of hills around Boston with mixed feelings. They must have wondered every day if the hour had arrived when Washington would attack the town and if he did, how the attack would come. Would he march his troops into the town? Would there be shooting in the streets? Would he simply surround Boston more and more closely and try to starve it out, starving friends as well as foes? Would he succeed in placing artillery on the hills beyond Roxbury Neck and would cannon balls crash into their houses?

These questions were answered on the fourth of March, 1776. For weeks before that night, secretly, though within a few miles of General Howe's army, supplies had been collected for an attack on the town. The house is still standing where much of the powder and shot were hidden. It is a square hip-roofed house with a central chimney. Near the road is a marker which reads:

This Tablet marks the Goddard Farm.
Here lived
1735   Hannah Seaver Goddard   1821
loyal Patriot · Wife of
1736   John Goddard   1816
Member of Committee of Safety
Wagon Master General · American Revolution.
Erected by
Hannah Goddard Chapter D.A.R.
Brookline · Massachusetts
1929

Cannon were hidden under the hay in the Goddard barn. In a smaller building opposite the house several hundred pounds of gunpowder were stored in the loft. A garrison of soldiers occupied this storehouse. They lived in the lower story. For weeks the Goddards waited for the signal to move the powder, knowing well that a single spark would destroy them all. Only a short distance across the fields lived a Tory family who often entertained British officers. At times these officers had ridden through the woods around the Goddard farm but they had never found anything to make them suspicious.

John Goddard, appointed Wagon Master General of Washington's army on August 9, 1775, was put in command of all the wagons that hauled material for the fortifications that General Washington had ordered built on Dorchester Heights. Joseph Goddard, a son of John, the wagon master, was a boy of fourteen at the time. He drove one of the teams under his father's orders. When he was an old man, he used to tell his grandchildren about that moonlight night in March 1776.

Before that night men had been busy in the woods of Dorchester and Milton cutting small slender trees for fascines. These were long bundles of sticks carefully bound together. In peacetime they might be used to strengthen the walls of a ditch or be placed along the edge of a road where there was danger of the sides caving in. For Washington's fortifications they were piled up along Dorchester Heights, two rows of them. The spaces between them were filled in with hay. The materials for this fortress wall were bulky but they were light and easily piled. After they were in place they were covered with earth.

All night long the ox teams hauled the fascines and the hay to the Heights. All night the wheels turned silently.

They were wrapped in hay to keep them quiet as they rolled slowly over the rutted cart tracks through the woods.

Not a whip was cracked, Joseph Goddard used to tell his grandchildren. There was not a shout or a call. "We touched the oxen sometimes with our ox goads to guide them left or right or to urge them to move ahead but it was all done in silence."

The moonlight must have shown a strange picture, one that General Howe, sleeping quietly in Boston, would never have dreamed of: the shadowy shapes of the great patient beasts tugging at the yokes, the men and boys in homespun trudging along beside them, the lurching wagons heaped with hay and fascines. Sometimes a load would seem to be only hay but through the hay could be dimly seen the shape of a cannon. Sometimes there were cannon balls under the hay or kegs of powder. Sometimes there were bullets for the long flintlock guns.

There were three hundred yoke of oxen under Mr. Goddard's orders that March night. When General Howe woke up the next morning, he was amazed by the sound of cannon fire from Dorchester Heights. He said the Americans had done more in one night than his soldiers could have done in six weeks. He and his army didn't stay long in Boston after that. On the seventeenth of March, St. Patrick's Day, the British Army left the town. There is still a parade in South Boston every year to celebrate that day. It ought to have oxen in it too in memory of John Goddard and his three hundred teams, but oxen have almost vanished from New England now.

When General Washington left Boston, he urged John Goddard to continue his service as wagon master but Mr. Goddard felt he could not leave his family and he returned to his Brookline farm. He was married twice and there was a family of sixteen children to bring up.

Once the second Mrs. Goddard was asked how she ever managed to bring up such a family.

She laughed and replied: "I put leather aprons on them and turned them out to play."

This plan seems to have worked well, as there were many successful and useful citizens among them.

"I get sort of confused about the Goddards and how they are related," Andrew said.

"I could confuse you even more," his grandmother said, "if I tried to tell you about all of John Goddard's sixteen children and their children in turn. Let's not bother too much about how they are all connected. What is interesting is how they lived."

A good many of the Goddards had red hair and what one Goddard wife described as "the angelic disposition that goes with it." Their hair was not powdered but brown or black or red, just as nature had given it to them. There probably never was a time when the difference between classes of people in America was so marked as it was just before the Revolution and during its early days. A Tory lady from Boston, almost filling the coach with her brocaded satin dress, almost touching the roof with her tall powdered wig, felt like a different kind of human being from the Brookline farmers' wives in their home-spun dresses of linsey-woolsey.

Fashionable Tory ladies, even if they had been born in America, considered themselves British and therefore entitled to look down on everyone else. In their eyes farmers and artisans belonged to the earth like potatoes or Roxbury pudding stone or old oak timbers. And so they did.

No doubt the farmers had rough hands, dirty a good deal of the time. Their faces were scorched by July suns and frostbitten by January blizzards. They wore clumsy boots made from the hides of their own cattle. The wool for their clothes grew on the backs of their own sheep and was dyed with the shucks of their own butternuts. Before wool could be grown, the fields where the sheep grazed had to be cleared of trees. Without their oxen the fields could not have been freed from stones and stumps. The oxen could not have been worked without ox yokes. So the Revolution depended on ox yokes. Only — how do you get an ox yoke if you haven't one? Well, if you are a Brookline farmer in 1776, you almost certainly do not get one ready-made in England. You have wood, the right kinds of wood, some flexible enough for the bows, some strong enough for the oxen to pull against. You also have a knife. You inherited it from your father. All you ever did to earn it was to make a new handle for it and to keep it sharp. All you need now is time for whittling. You have that on long winter evenings beside the fire. You also need patience, of course, but you would not be a farmer in Massachusetts if you did not have a pretty

good supply of that. It is no accident that the seal of the
Town of Brookline has on it — among other things — an
ox standing beside a plow.

More dangerous than either the British or American
bullets during the revolution was the epidemic of smallpox. It had never been so bad in America until the foreign troops brought it into the country. There had been
epidemics before, but now the disease spread so rapidly
that the whole country was in terror of it. Vaccination
was not yet practiced by doctors. In many places the only
treatment for smallpox was to take the patient to some
distant place, with someone who had had the disease to
nurse him, and to hang up a red flag to keep other people
away. After a while the patient either died or got well.
Dr. Aspinwall of Brookline did not know about vaccination but he did know about another treatment called inoculation which had been introduced into America half

a century before by Dr. Boylston, one of his Brookline neighbors.

When Dr. Aspinwall left the army, he decided to build a hospital on his Brookline farm so that patients in good health could come there and have the disease by inoculation. Inoculation is different from vaccination, which protects people against having smallpox itself. Inoculation actually gave them the disease but if they were well and strong at the time, had good nursing and medical care, they were likely to have the disease in a mild form or at least recover from it. Even with the best of care some of the patients died, but on the whole the experiment was a success. It was considered so much safer than taking a chance of having the smallpox naturally that whole families of children were sent to have smallpox by appointment.

Dr. Aspinwall soon had to build a second hospital and then a third. One of these buildings was where Perry Street runs into Aspinwall Avenue. The others were near where Longwood Station now stands. When vaccination was introduced into the country, about 1810, the need for inoculation ceased. Still, these hospitals of Dr. Aspinwall's were in a sense the beginning of the town's Health Service — the first attack on any disease with the idea that it is better to prevent it than to have to cure it. The buildings were taken down in 1803 and Dr. Aspinwall used some of the old timbers in a fine new house that he built for himself on Aspinwall Hill. The house had a columned porch and a tower above it and a beautiful rose garden.

"Was the tower like the one you used to live in?" asked Susie.

"No. The tower on the Aspinwall house was square. And if you'd like to see how it looked, just go to the window and look at Mr. Reid's house across the street and you'll see a copy of the old Aspinwall house, built many years later by one of his descendants."

"Right here on Hawthorn Road!" Susie exclaimed. "You mean that one I'm looking at?"

Her grandmother said yes and that it was quite a good copy of the old house. There was one thing, though, she told them, that could not very well be copied. A carpenter making some repairs to the roof of the old house noticed some names deeply cut in the beams. They were the names, sometimes with dates, sometimes with addresses from distant states, of the smallpox patients. Most of them, no doubt, returned safely to their homes but some lie buried in the Brookline marshes. It is all land now where the tides used to run and we may drive over the spot and not know that there were ever graves there.

It is hard to keep in mind how the tides rose and fell in Brookline at that time. Farmers had to think about the tides when they planned their haying. When tides were low, hay could be cut on the marsh land but there always came the extremely high tides of the fall. If rain came at the same time, any stacks of hay not already removed to higher ground would certainly be soaked and might even be carried away. The prudent farmers carried their hay to high ground early but there were always some who waited until the last minute. There was one stormy

Sunday when the meetinghouse was almost empty because most of the men of the congregation were down on the marsh trying to cart away their hay before the tide rose.

Churchgoing could be dangerous in Brookline in the eighteenth century. On another rainy Sunday — this one was in March — a great southerly storm had melted the snow and had turned the New Lane (Cypress Street) into a lake. Mr. Jackson, the minister, was ill that day and a Mr. Tappan from Cambridge was driving over to take his place in the pulpit. Mr. Tappan tried to drive his horse and chaise through the water but horse, chaise, the minister, and his son were all carried away by the flood. The son was nearly drowned but he managed to struggle out. His father sent him to get help and himself stayed in the water until he managed to unharness the horse. He then mounted the horse bareback, rode to the village, borrowed a saddle and rode back up Walnut Street to the Meeting House.

"This accident," says an old letter, "happened at first bell ringing. Mr. Tappan did not get to Mr. Jackson's till after the second began. He was so surprised and fatigued, that he could not give much account of himself, only he had been in the water.

"Mr. Jackson dressed the poor unfortunate man in a suit of his clothes, but as the smallclothes did not cover his knees, he was obliged to wear his own wet ones. He dried and fixed himself as well as he could and went clumping in to meeting in borrowed shoes just as Mr. Jackson had done his first prayer.

"Mr. Jackson's cloak was so short for him he could not look very buckish. Mr. Tappan had put his notes in his book and put them on the cushion behind him as he set out from Cambridge, but the current was so rapid that they were all carried off. Notwithstanding, he preached two excellent sermons from notes which he happened to have in his pocket."

"Were all Brookline people farmers?" Andrew asked. "Even the ministers?"

"Almost everyone except a minister had a farm, though he might do something else besides — run a chocolate mill or make cannon balls or saw lumber."

"Suppose you didn't want to be a farmer, would you have to be one just the same?"

"You had to be a pretty determined character to be anything else," his grandmother said. "If you'll get me the book about Nathaniel Goddard out of the trunk, I'll read you something about a boy who decided he didn't want to farm — if you'd like to hear it."

Andrew found the book and Susie got out her work, which was a bathing suit she was making for Janet's doll. Janet still had whooping cough but her doll was in fine health and really needed a suit for swimming. Andrew got out his work too. He was untangling a fishing line which had got itself into knots, the way fishing lines have always had a habit of doing, while he was fishing in Muddy River.

Nathaniel Goddard, their grandmother said, was the fourth son of John Goddard, the Wagon Master for Washington's army. John Goddard liked farming much better than being a wagon master and he wanted all his sons to be farmers or ministers. His oldest son, John Goddard, Jr., was sent to Harvard with the idea that he would become a minister. College education at that time was chiefly for ministers. Lawyers learned their profession by working for older lawyers. A young doctor learned his by riding around the country with an older doctor. No one seemed to think a teacher needed to learn how to teach. If he knew how to use a rattan cane and could read and write, he was considered well equipped. He didn't have to know how to spell because he had a spelling book. The teacher who taught the Goddard boys was not much of a speller. If a boy used most of the right letters in a word the teacher was satisfied. Especially if the boy was large and strong. He caned the small ones for any obvious mistakes.

John Goddard, Jr., was a disappointment to his father, because after receiving his Harvard education, he decided that he did not want to be a minister after all. He would have liked to be a doctor but his health was not especially good. He knew that the long rides on horseback far out into the country in all kinds of weather would be too hard for him so he decided to be an apothecary. In Portsmouth, New Hampshire, they needed an apothecary. Young John Goddard and a friend of his decided to open a shop there. Drugs were not available in this country — this was during the Revolution — so John sailed for Spain to buy a supply there.

He was captured twice by the British. He was placed on a prison ship where he was starved and grew so thin that he was able to escape through the porthole. He swam to an American ship but was soon captured again. This time he stayed a prisoner until he was exchanged. Prisoners could sometimes be released for exchange if someone would buy their freedom. John's father bought his. It took a long time for him to get home and though his mother had been thinking every day that he might come, when he arrived at last at the door of the house on Goddard Avenue he was so thin and starved looking that she did not know him. This experience did not dismay him and he did at last succeed in opening his shop in Portsmouth.

The second son, Joseph, liked farming and inherited the family farm on Goddard Avenue. The third son, Benjamin, liked farming too and he was a farmer most of his life but it was as a merchant that he earned the money to buy his Brookline estate. Mehitable lived in his house when she was a little girl.

Benjamin Goddard owned ships and sent cargoes to many parts of the world. Ships were often lost in those days, so that a voyage might have to be counted a complete failure. If it was successful, large profits might be made. At times the sale of a ship's cargo might bring more than the cost of the ship and the cargo and all the expenses of the voyage. Benjamin Goddard made so much on a single voyage that he retired from business when he was a little over forty, bought his Brookline farm, and managed it happily for the rest of his life.

The older John Goddard had helped these three older sons get started in the world by giving each of them a hundred pounds. At that time, during the Revolution and for some years after, Americans were still doing much of their figuring in pounds, shillings, and pence. However, they were starting to reckon in dollars too. A hundred pounds, in the old wagon master's way of figuring, was worth $333.33. This was to be each son's share but he could not expect to have it all in cash. He was supposed to take some of it, most of it if possible, in tools and stock or in things raised on the farm. His hundred pounds might really mean a young steer, or a colt, some chains, a plow, an axe, and other tools.

Every April, as soon as school was over, the Goddard boys began farm work. Nathaniel, the fourth boy, was a delicate child whose head ached violently whenever he stooped over. Most of his tasks — sowing seeds, weeding, picking up stones, digging dandelions, collecting small sticks and binding them into fagots, cutting and splitting wood, picking vegetables — meant stooping. He hated them all. The boys were not paid wages of course but they were sometimes allowed to earn a little money by raising chickens and selling the eggs or by selling herbs that they had grown. Nathaniel writes that he sometimes earned half a pistareen in this way.

A pistareen was a silver coin worth eighteen cents.

Probably because he disliked farming, Nathaniel was not a favorite with his father. His mother, however, was fond of him and praised him by saying: "Nathaniel was the best boy I ever knew. He was almost as good as a girl."

"Sounds pretty sissy," Andrew said.

"Don't decide about that until I finish telling you about how he got started in business," his grandmother said.

I think — she went on — that his mother meant that he was always willing to help her. With that big family — sixteen children — she never had much help. Sometimes there was a little bound girl who was supposed to help, but, as Nathaniel said, she was usually only a "help eat." Occasionally a woman came in to do washing and ironing. Sometimes a spinster came to spin the wool and flax and a little woman, almost a dwarf, named Nab Wilson did most of the Goddard weaving. That left for Mrs. Goddard only the cooking, baking, brewing, dishwashing, chamber work, cleaning, soap making, scouring and sanding floors, and taking care of sixteen children. In her spare time she made and mended clothes and knitted stockings. As soon as a child was six years old he had his work to do but there were always some children so small that they scrambled and crawled around in their leather aprons, which were called burvels.

One of the things that Nathaniel liked to do for his mother was to dye the yarn for the striped and checked shirts she made for him and his brothers. He would dye handkerchiefs too in the same kettle. First his mother, perhaps with Nab Wilson's help, made some rather coarse white linen. Then Nathaniel would take shot and tie it up in the linen, arranging it in any pattern that he chose, pulling the string tightly around each little bunch of shot. The linen was then put into the dye kettle. When it had been boiled for a while it was taken out and the strings were untied. This left a pattern of white rings where the string had been tied around the shot.

Nathaniel's father tried hard to discourage Nathaniel from going into business, always the boy's ambition. John Goddard had no confidence in his fourth son and would not give him any education that would help him. At last however he decided to allow Nathaniel to learn some kind of trade. So he first apprenticed the boy to a cabinetmaker. The cabinetmaker let his apprentice saw some mahogany logs and make some wooden pegs but before long he set him to work on his own farm where Nathaniel did much the same things he would have done at home. Mr. Goddard agreed with his son that this was no way to learn to make mahogany card tables. He took him away from the cabinetmaker's and apprenticed him to a jeweler, a Mr. Holmes.

The jeweler's shop was in Boston. It was July and Nathaniel was given a bed of straw in a garret under the eaves. The garret was like a furnace. There were two ragged blankets over the straw, which contained, Nathaniel said, enough fleas to meet an army and defeat it. He learned to make silver sleeve buttons and eyes for them so they could be sewn on. He engraved some letters on copper and he flattened out silver and planished it for spoons. Planishing is pounding with a special kind of hammer. The first thing he did every day was to sweep the shop. It had a dirt floor and the dirt he swept up was saved and heated. Any silver filings that were in it melted and ran together into a lump. Only a little was saved each day but, as Mr. Holmes kept saying, "My master swept his shop every day and in a few years he had saved enough for a tankard."

Nathaniel did not want to spend years sweeping up dirt until he got enough silver for a tankard. He still saw himself as a merchant with ships traveling to foreign ports. Besides he could not eat the food Mr. Holmes gave him. The jeweler economized in other ways besides saving silver filings. When farmers came to town with meat to sell, Mr. Holmes would wait until they were on their way home and then buy any odds and ends they had left. Since in those days no one had any ice to keep things cold, the meat soon spoiled. Nathaniel had come to try the jewelry business for two weeks to see if he liked it. At the end of a week he saw a familiar horse and wagon and his brother Joseph's face. He told Mr. Holmes he had decided not to be a jeweler, ran after the cart, jumped into it and rode home to Brookline.

Next he was apprenticed to his brother John, the one who was an apothecary in Portsmouth, New Hampshire. This was during the Revolution, and everyone was poor, but his mother fitted him out as well as she could. His father had a pair of leather breeches made for him but they turned out to be much too small. He had a striped wool and linen jacket with sleeves, two coarse linen shirts, bleached almost white with buttermilk. These were the first white shirts he had ever had. His mother had knitted him two pairs of blue socks and had made him a waistcoat of white homespun woven by Nab Wilson. He had a good pair of double-soled cowhide boots and a felt hat.

The hat looked all right when it was dry but when it was wet, the crown, Nathaniel said, rose up like a sugar loaf. To wear to meeting he had a secondhand cocked hat of the kind called a castor.

When he arrived in Portsmouth in this outfit, his brother took one look at him and had a tailor make him a pair of black wool breeches. They gave the tailor the leather ones as part payment. The white waistcoat they had dyed black, but the dye was not very good and the black used to come off on his white shirts.

Nathaniel learned a good deal about business in Portsmouth. His brother sold not only drugs but also wine, dried and fresh fruits, tea — at nine shillings a pound — other groceries, ironware, and in fact, Nathaniel said, everything generally kept for sale in the town.

"Why, it was something like a drugstore now!" Susie said. "Only no ice cream, I suppose."

"No comic books," Andrew observed.

No — his grandmother said — and if there had been any, Nathaniel would not have had time to read them. He was kept busy pounding drugs in a mortar with an iron pestle that weighed thirteen and a half pounds, binding up cut fingers, weighing out medicines and groceries, or measuring off cloth. He was learning all the time but retail trade did not really interest him. He still wanted to be a merchant. It was while he was in Portsmouth that he made his first trading venture.

He had eight dollars, his life savings, earned half a pistareen at a time. He gave it all to a sea captain to invest for him. The captain, when he came back to Portsmouth months later, had forgotten all about Nathaniel's eight dollars. He was not a dishonest man, just careless. The result was not very different but he good-naturedly gave the boy a basket of tangerine oranges, which he had really intended to give away as presents to his friends. Nathaniel sold them for twenty-five cents apiece and made fifty dollars. This clothed him for several years, he said. As an apprentice he received no wages and indeed his brother was paid by their father for Nathaniel's food and the amount was taken out of his inheritance.

His next apprenticeship brought him a little nearer to his dream of being a merchant. This time his master was a storekeeper and shipowner in Boston. Nathaniel had hoped to learn bookkeeping but his work turned out to be mostly taking care of his master's horse and piling boards on the wharf before loading them on a ship. Still, he did learn something about trade. Money seldom changed hands. They would trade boards, salt pork, or butter for logwood chips from Campeche to be used in making dyes, or for rum, sugar, or molasses. Some of the prices at which they traded were: clear boards at twenty-six shillings a thousand feet, butter at fivepence a pound, New England rum at a shilling and sixpence a gallon, molasses at a pistareen for half a gallon.

Part of his work was to stand at the door of the shop and call out, "What have you got to sell?" He also cut up pork, made barrels to put it in, tried out lard, made bricks and sold them at three dollars a thousand. He was clever with tools and he built a rack for horses. He made gateposts, a trough for kneading dough, and whittled out a stick to stir the hasty pudding.

"What's that?" Andrew asked.

"Corn-meal mush," his grandmother said. "You made it by stirring corn meal into water and cooking it till it was thick enough for the pudding stick to stand up straight in it. When it would stand, the pudding was called 'lawful pudding.' It was against the law to feed it to your apprentices if it was any thinner. You ate it — if you were lucky — with butter and molasses."

"Ugh!" said Andrew.

I am inclined to agree with you — his grandmother said — but it was a treat to Nathaniel to have molasses or butter. Things were getting better for him. He was beginning to earn money. He worked on the widening of Boston Neck, that narrow strip of land that was then the only connection between Boston and Roxbury and the rest of North America. When the tide was low, he worked on a sea wall built of Roxbury pudding stone. When the wall was at last completed, they filled in between it and the Neck with clay. They worked on the wall from half ebb tide to half flood tide every day. When the widening was finished, they set out elms along the road.

Nathaniel's wages were eight dollars a week and his master was supposed to give him clothes, but this did not include such things, necessary in those days, as knee and shoe buckles, sleeve buttons, and neck cloths. His greatest hardship at that time, he said, was that he was allowed only one clean shirt a week. He often got so wet at his work that he was never really dry except when he put on his clean shirt on Sunday and went to meeting.

At last he thought he had learned enough so that he could go into business for himself. His father still thought that he had no skill for it and was bound to fail. Yet Nathaniel felt sure that he had learned something of people's needs. He knew that he must buy cheap and never sell at less than cost and he was bound, he says, "to live on my own earnings and not another's."

His mother did not think that he would fail but she would say to him, "Don't be impatient. Something will turn up," and Nathaniel would reply, "Perhaps, ma'am, but not unless I turn it up."

He was determined to go to "the Eastward." That meant to Maine, which was still part of Massachusetts. At last his father agreed to help him. He helped his son raise the sum of one hundred and twenty pounds, borrowing from among their Brookline neighbors. He also gave him, as part of his one-hundred-pound inheritance, some salt pork, corn, lard, and vinegar. The whole amount of Nathaniel's capital added up to $566.60.

With some of his borrowed money Nathaniel bought more corn, corn meal, tea, molasses, linen and cotton cloth, tinware, teapots, pewter, shot and musket balls. For use in his shop he bought a set of scales and measures. For himself he bought a mattress and blankets. He sailed in March, 1789, for the Eastward and reached Mount Desert in four days. He must have been glad as he sailed in past the purple bronze cliffs of Iron Bound Island and came into calm waters, for he had been seasick all the way. The first food he had was a drink of switchell, a mixture of molasses and water.

At last they reached Passamaquoddy Bay. Nathaniel rented a store fronting Harbor de Lue in Campobello. The rent was eight dollars a month and the store was so small that he kept his mattress half in a small passage that led to the store and half in the store itself. Until May there were days when snow came through the cracks in the building and blew in over his lumpy mattress. He slept in his clothes. He could not afford to buy wood at a dollar a cord so he picked up driftwood from the beach. It was often wet and did not burn very well.

His customers were British troops disbanded after the Revolution, Tory refugees from the colonies, roving Indians, and English convicts. His food was dried fish, ship's bread, Indian meal and salt pork. He was not much of a cook, he says, and the hasty pudding he made "tasted like what I used to feed to my father's hogs and chickens. If I had earned anything that day, I used a little molasses. I drank cold water from the spring. I slept with a loaded musket by my side."

The musket was to prevent the theft of his goods by his customers. It worked pretty well at night but it did not keep the customers from stealing things around the store by day when he was busy. However, by charging the same price to everyone, by taking whatever the customers brought in trade at a fair price, he began to get ahead. Some of the things he took in trade were cod, pollock, herring, fish oil, blubber, shingles, old iron, old swords, muskets, pewter, furs and moose hides, feathers and grindstones, cheese and clapboards. Once he bought a beautifully ornamented horseman's pistol from Captain Charles Storrow, who had used it in the West Indies. In fact Nathaniel took whatever came his way and shipped his strange collection of goods back to his brother Benjamin in Boston. Benjamin was still in business and he kept Nathaniel supplied with new goods for his store.

By the end of the first year Nathaniel had increased his property to $1000. Soon he had six people working for him, including a woman to cook. He no longer had to make that hasty pudding that tasted like chickenfeed. Now he could be away from the store sometimes and go on trading voyages along the coast. He built a new store, doing much of the work himself. He had some help from an old mason whose favorite expression was: "Odds fakins, rabbit my catskins!" Nathaniel had to show him how to build the fireplace and the old man was so pleased with the plan for it that he said, "Odds fakins, rabbit my catskins, if you haven't done it!"

In the new store there was still trouble about goods being stolen by the customers. He had to pitch one drunken, noisy Indian, who had attacked him, down six or seven steps. Once he had a battle with six or seven Indians who had stolen things. He made them give the things back. One of them tried to shoot him but a squaw pulled the gun aside just in time. This was the last battle. He had won. He says: "I always made up my mind, never gave up to them, always dealt with them on the same terms as white customers, taught them to respect me."

He stayed there seven years. He liked the place. The climate of the Bay of Fundy was mild in winter, cool in summer. He liked the pleasant rivers flowing into the Bay, liked to see grampus spouting, seals diving, and shoals of fish swimming up to his front door, ready to be caught. He could light a fire at night, he said, and the herring would come in such numbers that he could dip them up in pails. He could count a hundred fishing boats around Campobello in the season.

When Nathaniel left, he turned the business over to a Colonel Trescott, who was, he says, "part of the noblest work of God, an honest man." That first little shop, where he had slept with the snow drifting in over him, was the foundation of a great fortune. When he came back to Boston, he was, he says, "an old bachelor and pretty well qualified to be a hermit." He was not a very old bachelor — twenty-nine — but he had hardly spoken to a civilized person for seven of those years. He did not remain a bachelor long. He married and built in Summer Street in Boston a beautiful house of pink Philadelphia brick.

There were green lawns and gardens around his house. Horse chestnut trees shaded it and honeysuckle twined around its white pillars. There was a green fence around the grounds. He liked this color. His ships, which went from Boston Harbor all over the world, were painted green below the waterline and ivory above. One was all green and when it appeared in Canton, the Chinese called it *The Green Dragon*.

Nathaniel Goddard's house was one of the sights of the

city. It used to be pointed out to visitors along with the
State House and the Old South Church. He and his wife
brought up their eleven children there and always welcomed their friends with a kindness and hospitality long
remembered. Managing Summer Street, Mrs. Goddard
said, was like running a hotel. Frequently they drove out
to Brookline in their comfortable two-wheeled chaise to
see Benjamin. They would often find when they came
home again that the front hall was full of trunks and
bags belonging to some member of the family who had
dropped in for a visit.

Perhaps the chaise took Mr. Goddard only as far as his
counting house where he got news of his ships from many
ports. The list reads like a geography — Dublin, Lisbon,
London, St. Petersburg, Le Havre, Cuba, Antwerp, Java,
Liverpool, Charleston, Surabaya, New Orleans, Hamburg, Samarang, Amsterdam, and many others. His
letters to his captains show how well he knew these faraway places to which he had sailed only in his imagination. One captain is sailing to Batavia in the East Indies
and Mr. Goddard writes: "Do not let the men drink
water in Batavia: it is good in the rest of the island but
not there."

He knew where the best coffee and hemp and sheeting
and iron could be bought and where would be the best
chance to sell cotton and tobacco. When the ships came
home there would be presents for everyone. Once there
were seven gold watches, one for each of his daughters.
Another time there was a piano, a harp, and a lyre, so that
there could be music at Summer Street in the evenings

when the Brookline relatives dropped in.

After the music, there would be bowls of nuts and raisins and decanters of Madeira brought back from the island in one of the Goddard ships. By this time Nathaniel entertained his guests dressed as he was to be for the rest of his life. He was a rosy faced, gray haired man of medium height, stout but standing erect and as quick in his movements as he was when he battled half a dozen Indians. He wore a black coat of an old fashioned cut, knee breeches with silver buckles, a high neck cloth and a ruffled shirt frill, very white and crisp looking. In winter he wore a black waistcoat. His friends could tell that summer had come when they saw him in a white one. His hair was worn in a queue and tied with a black silk ribbon. He always wore silk stockings, which were imported for him, six pairs every year. He was slightly lame from a fall he got once in unloading a ship in Passamaquoddy Bay.

He worked hard all his life. Besides his business as a merchant he was president of a bank and he helped to organize an insurance company. It was partly because of his style of dress that the insurance business was known as the Ruffled Shirt Office.

When he retired from the bank he wrote to one of his nephews that "if by working sixteen hours a day, appropriating seven hours to sleep and one to amusement and eating, I cannot get money, I will go without it."

At one time he lost large sums of money because of the business failures of others, but when he was over seventy years old he set out to repay every debt and did so. He died in 1853 when he was eighty-six years old. He was, to use his own words, "that best part of the work of God, an honest man." He was also a kind and generous one. He had been fortunate, he felt, especially in his family, who had been his best friends.

When he wrote his recollections he said: "I had in early life a kind mother. I have yet living a kind brother [this was Benjamin Goddard] who came forward and relieved me in my distress."

It must have made him happy to get Michael to attach the horse to the chaise and lead him round to the door and drive out to Brookline to see Benjamin, and to see their mother who lived at Benjamin's in the square yellow house on the turnpike when the oval flower beds were all in their pride with tulips and narcissus. Though one of the brothers was a merchant and the other a farmer, they were the same kind of men, honorable, just, generous, sensible. Among Nathaniel Goddard's papers was one on which he had written down some of the principles by which he had lived. There are good sayings among them, about exercise and temperance and habit, about going ahead alone when you know you are right no matter what other people think, about keeping silent if you have nothing good to say. Still, I think his best remark was the one he made to his mother when she told him that something would turn up: "Perhaps so, Ma'am, but not unless I turn it up."

"You don't still think he was a sissy, do you, Andrew?"

"Odds fakins, rabbit my catskins, no!" said Andrew.

IF YOU WERE a boy or a girl between 1730 and 1775, you would have been a subject of two British kings — George II and George III. You would have done your arithmetic in pounds, shillings, and pence. If your spelling was like that on old papers of the day, like some belonging to the Sharp family of Brookline, you spelled pretty much as you pleased.

The Sharp family owned a large amount of land along what is now Harvard Street. Their land went as far as Park Street in one direction and as far as the Longwood marshes along the Muddy River in the other. Captain Robert Sharp used much of this land to pasture cattle. During the years before the Revolution Boston had so many new houses built along its streets and lanes that there was not enough land for cow pastures. Cows could still be seen lying on the Common but people who owned a large number of cattle often sent some of them out to Brookline for Captain Sharp to board. Captain Sharp kept careful accounts. He sold cider — which he spelled "Sider" — as well as feeding cattle. He usually had to take something in trade for it, perhaps "naels" or a "grenston." Once he allowed his customer two shillings and eightpence for four "orringes" and another time ten pence for one "orring." Oranges were a great luxury, as they were when Nathaniel Goddard made his first trading venture, because they were all brought from overseas.

Captain Sharp also kept careful accounts of what he spent himself. He bought some new clothes one year and made a list of them. It reads in £. s. d.:

"Excuse me, Grandma," Susie said, "what does £. s. d. mean?"

"Pounds, shillings, and pence."

"Yes, but that doesn't match. It ought to be P. s. p."

Her grandmother told her that £. s. d. are symbols representing the Latin words librae, solidi, denarii.

"Here," she went on, "is what Captain Sharp got for his £. s. d."

Paid Thomas Sharle for Cloas

	£.	s.	d.
For a hatt	3.	3.	0
For a shurt	0.	9.	0
For Britches		15.	0
For stockens		3.	6
For a coat	2.		

If we call a pound $3.33, as John Goddard did, it would make the clothes cost about twenty dollars, half of which was for a hat. Probably that means that the hat was imported from England. The other things could be made of American wool and linen.

At about the same time there is a receipt signed by the schoolteacher. She was paid £3 16s. for teaching school one term. She would have had to work most of the term to earn enough to buy a man's hat but luckily for her and for the town she of course made her own bonnets, braiding the straw for them first. She was satisfied if she got enough money to buy food. Another Brookline teacher used to wear her good long-skirted dress to school but changed into a short dress when she got there and hung the long one carefully behind the door. In this way her best dress lasted her for many years.

With such salaries it is not surprising that teachers were not always especially well educated and that they did not always spell according to the spelling book. One of the Brookline teachers presented the following bill to the town:

"The town of Brookline Depttor to Mary Bowen for keeping school fore months from the seventh of June 1760 at twenty six shillings and eaight pence per month — £5. 6.sh. 8d."

However she did spell a little better than the mason who made some repairs on the old school house at the center of the town.

His bill reads:

December ye 6. 1758
to work don at the Skul hous
to shinggeling the ruf and finding 15 shingels,
    and nales and Lime to pint it   *1. 1. 0*
to laying the harth and finding 60 bricks and
    wheling 12 whelborrers of Durt to Ras it   *2.*
lathing and plastern Severl plases   *0. 1. 0*
                                     4. 0. 0

Moses Scott

Mr. Scott's arithmetic was almost as strange as his spelling. The selectmen looked the bill over carefully, found it was incorrect, and paid him only ten shillings and eightpence for all his shingling, laying bricks, plastering, and wheeling barrows full of dirt.

However, the selectmen were in a more generous mood when a new minister was ordained in 1775. The whole bill for the ordination dinner came to over £18. It included such items as Rum, Sugar, Spice, Turces (which probably means turkeys), fouls, pork, crambres, and puding pans. Unfortunately this minister was not satisfactory and in a few years they had to spend twenty-four pounds to ordain Mr. Jackson. Crambres (cranberries) were served at this dinner too and also butter, eggs, cakes, "pickels," and "Ross water," which I suppose means rose water, a favorite flavoring at the time for cakes and puddings.

At the same time there were some repairs made on the meetinghouse. The pulpit was raised, a new floor and steps up to it were built. Locks, hinges, and nails were supplied. There was a new door made and some painting done. The whole thing came to less than five pounds. It was the custom to write at the bottom of a bill "Except errors" or "Errors excepted." These phrases meant that the man who presented the bill considered the bill correct but that the selectmen must check it and make sure it was right. The carpenter who repaired the pulpit was another original speller. He wrote at the bottom of his bill "Except Arrows."

The expenses of the town of Brookline in the eighteenth century were chiefly for the church and the schools. There were few roads, no sidewalks, no street lights, no fire or public water supply, no collection of trash and garbage. Houses were widely scattered. They were usually unpainted. Captain Sharp's house, a better and bigger house than most in the town, had the window frames painted white but the walls were unpainted during the two centuries it stood. It weathered to a dark brown that was almost black and the white frames seemed to make the windows stare out from the dark walls.

Most houses of the time were small one story and a half buildings with no paint at all. Paint was imported from England and was expensive. The British did not encourage the colonists to set up factories of their own. The colonies were regarded as natural markets for British manufactures such as paper, window glass, painters' colors, and finely woven fabrics. In exchange they wanted the American fish, furs, timber, and tobacco.

In a flourishing port such as Boston there were, of course, rich merchants who lived in handsome houses of brick and painted wood. People in English clothes of satin and brocade and fine broadcloth strolled along the Mall on the Common on fine spring evenings. The ladies appeared in their widely hooped skirts and the men in long coats and waistcoats reaching almost to their knees. Both wore powdered wigs and silk stockings and buckles on their shoes. The men wore swords at their sides. Either might be wearing lace ruffles that would cost more than a Brookline schoolteacher could earn in a year. A Brookline minister might live for a year and bring up his family on less than the value of the clothes a Boston merchant and his wife might wear to church.

These fine ladies and gentlemen would drive along the muddy roads of Brookline, occasionally stopping at the Punch Bowl to bait their horses.

"Baiting horses! I thought bait was for fish," Andrew remarked.

"It means to rest the horses, to rub them down, to give them water and perhaps some oats. In the meantime the man would have a bowl of the famous punch and his wife might condescend to drink some tea."

There were beginning to be other houses around the village — she added — but it must have seemed like a very humble little settlement to fashionable Bostonians. If they thought about Brookline at all except as a bad road on the way to Cambridge, they probably considered it as a convenient place to pasture cattle. They would have been much surprised to learn that it would ever be anything more than a wood lot and a cow pasture for Boston.

However, by 1740 there were a few fine houses in Brookline and one of them, part of which is older than 1740, still stands — the Zabdiel Boylston house. It is on Fisher Hill opposite the old Reservoir. When the early part of the house was built, the Reservoir was still a meadow, lower than the old Sherburne Trail which ran along it. The Worcester Turnpike at this point still follows in a general way the line of the old Indian trail. By the time the Boylston house was built, the trail had been gradually widened from a footpath to a coach road. That is, a coach could move along slowly if it didn't sink into a mudhole.

Dr. Thomas Boylston, a surgeon in King Philip's War, came to live on this Brookline hilltop in 1665 and there brought up his family of twelve children in a house which is now part of the Fisher Hill house. One of his daughters married John Adams of Braintree. Their son, John Adams, became the second President of the United States. The best-known member of the Boylston family was Thomas Boylston's son Zabdiel. He became a doctor and it was through his work that Dr. William Aspinwall and other American doctors learned about inoculation for smallpox. Dr. Boylston was the first one to use inoculation to fight the disease.

In 1721 there was a terrible epidemic of smallpox in Boston. More than a sixth of the patients died and those who recovered were badly disfigured. It was the Reverend Cotton Mather who told Dr. Boylston about a report by the Royal Society in England on smallpox. The Royal Society studied all kinds of scientific subjects.

Many of the most scholarly men in England belonged to the Society and membership in it was considered a great honor. In one of the papers read before the members there was an account of how smallpox was treated in Turkey. While a patient was in good health, the doctor would scrape a little skin from his arm, rub a little smallpox virus into the raw spot, and cover it with a nut shell. It was claimed that patients who were inoculated in this way seldom died and that most of them had the disease in such a mild form that they were not badly disfigured. No one had tried inoculation in England when Dr. Boylston began his experiments. All the other doctors to whom the idea was suggested opposed it violently. They called it a crime and said it was in a class with poisoning. Yet Dr. Boylston went on. He inoculated himself first, then one of his children. Both had the disease lightly and recovered.

Ministers preached sermons against him and wrote pamphlets to arouse people against inoculation. They argued that smallpox was sent by God as a punishment for the sins of the people and that to try to stop it would only "provoke him the more."

The inhabitants of Boston and of the neighboring towns became so excited when they heard that Dr. Boylston was actually practicing inoculation that men patrolled the streets carrying ropes so that when they caught the criminal, they could promptly hang him from the nearest tree. For fourteen days Dr. Boylston had to hide in his own house. Only his wife knew the hiding place. The house was searched several times. Sometimes the seekers came by day, sometimes by night, but they never found him. One evening while Mrs. Boylston and the children were sitting together in the parlor, someone dashed a hand grenade through the window. Luckily the fuse was knocked off against a piece of furniture and the family escaped death.

For some time the doctor could not appear in public. He used to steal out at night in disguise and visit his patients. The hours while he was gone must have seemed very long to his wife. Until he was safely back in his hiding place again, she must have anxiously followed in her mind the dark roads and bridlepaths and cartways where he was riding. She must have seen in her imagination how he would quiet his horse and tie him in the shadows away from the lighted windows of the house where the sick person was waiting for him; how he would stand still in the darkness, listening, until he was sure that there was no one near the house, then muffle his face in his old cloak, move slowly across a dark field, and tap softly on the door.

Or perhaps there was a patient in the city dying of smallpox. The doctor would have to find his way there through dark alleys. He could not carry a lantern because he might be seen. He would be safe only when he was inside the house. Even men who were anxious to get a rope around his neck would not dare to enter a house where there was smallpox. Dr. Boylston seems to have had all kinds of courage. Whether it takes more courage to run the risk of being set upon by an angry mob and hanged, or to face a dangerous disease, or to follow an unpopular experiment where a failure will make you a criminal, is hard to tell. But surely, Dr. Boylston was a brave man, ready to do his duty as a doctor, no matter what risks he ran.

In spite of threats of violence he went on with his experiments. He inoculated two of his servants. Both recovered after light cases of the disease. However, the Boston authorities summoned him and accused him of wrongdoing. He was questioned severely and rebuked. He continued to be threatened and insulted but he went on inoculating patients who asked to be protected against the disease. During the year that smallpox raged in Boston, he inoculated two hundred and eighty-six patients. They were of all ages — small babies, children, young men and women, middle-aged people, grandmothers and grandfathers. Six of them died. During the same year there were 5759 cases of "natural" smallpox in Boston. Of these 844 died.

The opposition to inoculation still continued in Boston but in England there was great interest in Dr. Boylston's experiments. He was invited by Sir Hans Sloane, the court physician, to visit London. He accepted the invitation and stayed there a year and a half. While he was in London, he was made a Fellow of the Royal Society. He was one of the first Americans to receive this honor and be able to write F.R.S. after his name.

When he retired from his profession he became one of Brookline's leading farmers. He rebuilt and enlarged the old house on Fisher Hill. It is now much as he left it, with its hip roof, beautiful doorway, and the old paneled door with the long strap hinges.

It was the first house I ever saw that had window seats or tiles around the fireplace. Our own fireplace at the time was the last word in elegance — it was white marble, snowy, and cold and had bunches of grapes around it, but somehow I liked the old tiles in the Boylston house and the wooden moldings and the panels above the fireplace.

Dr. Boylston bred horses on his farm and trained them himself. When he was more than eighty-four years old, he was seen in Boston riding a fine colt he was breaking to the saddle. He lived to see inoculation widely used and accepted. Vaccination, when it came, was a much safer protection than inoculation against smallpox, but if it had not been for Dr. Boylston's courage in experimenting with inoculation, the same violent and ignorant opposition might have been made to vaccination. Many lives were saved by inoculation. Many more by vaccination. The credit for the idea of protection against one of the most terrible of diseases must go to this brave man.

He is buried in the Walnut Street Cemetery and this is his epitaph:

"Sacred to the memory of Zabdiel Boylston Esq. and F.R.S. who first introduced the practice of inoculation into America. Through a life of extensive benevolence he was always faithful to his word, just in his dealings, affable in his manners, and after a long sickness in which he was exemplary for his patience and resignation to his maker, he quitted this mortal life in a just expectation of a happy immortality, March Ist. 1776."

Like the old eighteenth-century ladies who lived on until the nineteenth and were interesting figures to Edward Atkinson, there are still old houses standing in Brookline to remind us of days before the Revolution. It used to be the custom to call any old house colonial. Actually, of course, they were not colonial unless they were built when Massachusetts was still a colony. The Boylston house is truly colonial and so is the Edward Devotion house, an interesting house because of its connection with some of the earliest settlers of the town. One of them became the town's first benefactor. Brookline was still called Muddy River and was part of Boston when the Devotions came there. Edward Devotion, Jr., in whose honor the school near which the old house stands was named, inherited about seventy-six acres of land in the town from his father and bought other pieces of property there. The school and the old house both stand on what was once part of the Devotion homestead. The younger Edward held several town offices. He was surveyor of roads, a constable, a fence viewer, a hog reeve, and a grand juryman. His wife had a seat on the fore seat of the meetinghouse.

A front seat in meeting meant that the Devotion family had a position of some importance in the town. There was nothing democratic about the way the seats were assigned. The best people — that is the most prosperous and respectable people — had the best seats. However, the Devotions were not impressive enough for Edward Devotion to be called Mister or Esquire. These titles

were reserved for the real leaders of the community. The
older Devotion was referred to as "Goodman Devotion"
by Judge Samuel Sewall in his diary. Judge Sewall owned
land in Brookline and he used to bait his horse at Goodman Devotion's on his way through the town.

When Edward Devotion, Jr., died in 1744, he gave to
"the Church of Christ in Brookline a silver tankard con-
taining one quart." After arranging for several other
legacies, he left the following instructions:

"Item: In case my estate prove to be sufficient to pay
my just debts and funeral charges and the afore mentioned legacies, and should there be any overplus left,
then my will is and I hereby give said overplus to the
Town of Brookline towards building or maintaining a
school as near the centre of said town as shall be agreed
to by the town."

There proved to be enough money in the estate to pay
the debts and legacies so when Edward Devotion's affairs
were settled in 1762, Brookline received £15 4d. lawful
money for the purchase of a silver tankard and also
"308½ Johannes, full weight" for use of the school. The
Johannes were gold coins.

We have the inventory of his estate and it is interesting
to see what property one of the more prosperous citizens
of Brookline owned in the middle of the eighteenth
century:

15 acres of land	*£ 310*
7 " " "	*105*
1 negrow	*30*

Waring apparell	*20*
Beds and bedding	*40*
Tables, chairs, wooden wear	*20*
puter, iron, brass	*25*
1 iron bar	*25*

"Memo: There is sundry Bonds due sd. estate with interest. £1735.6.6. old tenor. Beside some desperate Bonds amounting to £537. Cash, old tenor, £80.15."

Edward Devotion, Jr., could read and write enough to sign his name to some earlier documents but the will is signed with his mark. Perhaps he was too ill at the time to write.

The money he gave to the town for school purposes was used toward paying a teacher. At the rate teachers were paid it must have lasted for some years. It is certainly appropiate that one of our fine Brookline schools should be named after him.

The old Putterham School on Newton Street gives some idea of what an eighteenth-century school building was like. The oldest part of it was probably built before 1768 and it is standing where it originally stood. During the early part of the nineteenth century it was enlarged and improved several times. The lot of land on which the first building stood was so small — twenty by thirty feet — that when the town decided to enlarge the building in 1839, they first had to buy more land.

"Putterham is a funny name," Andrew said.

"Yes," said his grandmother. "When I was a little girl, there was an idea that everyone who lived near Putterham Marsh used to putter around. And that's how the place got its name. Ham was an old word meaning town or village. Actually there were very few houses near it and I don't remember seeing anyone even doing anything as energetic as puttering around there. It was all marshy land, with clumps of trees growing out of it here and there. We used to go there to skate."

I was always a very poor skater — she went on — partly from natural lack of talent and partly because of the skates of the day, which clamped onto the shoes and never seemed to fit. I don't remember seeing a good pair of shoe skates until I was practically grown up. On an open pond — like Hammond's Pond, for instance — I was hopeless, either falling down or standing shivering on the edge. Putterham just suited me because I could follow little icy paths through the trees. I could always catch hold of a branch if my skate came off and I was going to fall.

My brother and I also used to skate on a marshy little pond called Cowand's Pond where Lee and Warren Streets now meet. It has been drained and filled in for many years now and there are houses and green lawns where we used to skate. It was so shallow that we could go there alone and fall in all we liked. We decided to entertain our friends, about four of them, and we saved our money for weeks until we had enough to buy a quart of Vogel's ice cream and some of the macaroons that they baked every day.

We chose a good cold day, so the ice cream wouldn't melt, walked a mile and a half to get it, then a little more than that to the pond. Our friends were there waiting. We served ice cream right out of the carton with Bushway's spoons from our collection. It was strawberry and we ate it RIGHT ON THE ICE. One of the friends we invited declined on the ground that it was "the silliest thing she ever heard." Perhaps it was, but I still remember how good it tasted and I have always considered that if you really want to enjoy ice cream, you should eat it on skates.

Putterham Marsh has been drained too now and is part of the Brookline Golf Course but when the Goddards used to go to Putterham School, they must have gone there to slide when the marsh was frozen. Skates were an unusual possession in Revolutionary times. You hear about children coasting and sliding but not about their skating. Probably when Nathaniel Goddard first went to school, he was too small even for sliding. The thing he remembered best about school was how he and his brothers got their dinners.

At first they took bread and meat from home. After a short time their father and mother decided that the children should have a hot meal in the middle of the day. The result was what must surely have been one of the first Hot Lunch Programs in American school history. Mrs. Goddard arranged witth Nab Wilson, that strange-looking little woman, four feet high, with a black beard and thick legs, to let the schoolmistress use the fire in Nab's house for cooking. This house, where Nab wove wool and linen for the neighbors, was only a pitched roof over a cellar, but it had a chimney and a fireplace and she kept her fire going in cold weather. The Goddard boys picked up sticks in the woods nearby for fuel and the schoolmistress helped them make hot chocolate over the fire. Of course there was no stove. They brought from home an iron skillet, some pewter basins, and some pewter spoons. Nathaniel says he thinks they may have had some molasses or sugar to sweeten the chocolate but that he did not remember any such luxury. Since unsweetened chocolate is exceedingly bitter, it seems that he would have remembered the flavor if it were served without sweetening. Probably they had at least a little molasses in it.

Nathaniel's books — she added — were a primer, a speller, and a Bible, but he did not learn to read the Bible until later. He says that a boy who could read the Bible with "a good tone" was much of a scholar. He learned later to write a fine hand, as his account books and letters show.

All the time that Nathaniel was growing up he heard talk about liberty. Liberty was not, of course, a new idea in New England. The Pilgrims came to Plymouth and the Puritans to Salem and Boston and other Massachusetts towns because they wanted to worship God in their own way. Other settlers came because they were eager to have land of their own, to be able to shoot a deer or a partridge without being considered a criminal, to work hard and be able to leave to their children a better world than they had known themselves. As a rule they were poor people. Rich and lazy and contented people did not cross the ocean to wrestle with the forests and rocks and swamps of New England.

It is hard to say just when the farmers of a town like Brookline began to think of themselves as Americans, but they certainly did so by 1768. The Hultons, who lived in Brookline at that time, were a Tory family. Miss Hulton kept a diary and one day in 1768 she wrote that "the Sons of Liberty were howling like Indians." This was un-English behavior she felt. She said that English mobs were much better mannered.

It was probably a good deal of fun to go out on a dark evening and howl like an Indian under Tory windows — so much fun that it is just possible that Miss Hulton's Sons of Liberty may really have been grandsons. The real Sons of Liberty were earnest men who resented commercial and political tyranny as strongly as their ancestors had resented religious tyranny. They were probably sitting quietly at home around the fire with their neighbors, making plans to work with other towns to have unfair taxes repealed, appointing committees of correspondence, and writing out resolutions.

On December 15, 1767, the inhabitants of the Town of Brookline assembled at the meetinghouse and voted that "the town will take all prudent and legal methods to promote industry, economy, and manufactures in this Province and in any of the British American colonies and will likewise take all legal measures to discourage the use of European superfluities."

European superfluities included paint, paper, glass, and tea, all of which were taxed. After a time, because of the American protests, customs duties were repealed on everything but the tea. The duty on tea was kept as a matter of principle — to show that the British parliament could levy whatever taxes it thought right. With the Americans it was a matter of principle too. They decided that no parliament had a right to levy taxes without the consent of the taxpayers. Since they were not represented in parliament, they were determined not to pay the tax. There were Englishmen who agreed with them, but King George and his ministers did not listen to them.

In 1772 John Goddard was named as one of a Brookline committee to correspond with committees from other towns. That same year this little group of perhaps fifty farm families issued a Bill of Rights. So far Brookline and the other towns had used no methods that were not "legal and prudent." A change was coming over the minds of even the most serious and law-abiding citizens. By December 1773 feeling had reached a point where the Americans of Boston had decided that no tea should be landed at their port. The British commander of armed men-of-war lying in the harbor said that if the Americans did not withdraw their opposition to the landing of the tea, it would be forced ashore "under cover of the cannon's mouth."

On the sixteenth there was a meeting at a Boston church to decide what to do to prevent the landing of the tea. A committee from the meeting went to consult the Governor of the Province — Governor Hutchinson. He put them off, saying he would answer them at five o'clock. When they went back at five, they learned that the

Governor had gone to his country house at Milton without giving them an answer. When the men heard this, the meeting broke up. There were shouts of "Let every man do his duty and be true to his country!" and "Huzza for Griffin's wharf!"

Griffin's Wharf was where the three ships, loaded with the East India Company's tea, were lying surrounded by British men-of-war. The plans for the most famous tea party ever held had been made so quietly that no one knew them or knows now who first suggested it or who took part in it. Yet somehow each man who rushed from the meeting and disguised himself as an Indian knew he would not be alone.

That we know anything definite about the tea party is largely because of an account given by one of the "Indians," George Robert Twelvetrees Hewes, when he was an old man.

It was dark by the time the figures in Indian clothes, faces blackened with coal dust, hatchets in their hands, began to meet others disguised in the same way in the street. They did not recognize each other. If they suspected who the others were, they did not call them by name as they marched toward Griffin's Wharf. Three men took command and all obeyed them. They divided the Indians into three parties, about twenty in each. They boarded all three ships at the same time.

Hewes was told by the commander of his party to go to the captain of the ship and demand the keys to the hatches and half a dozen candles. The captain gave them to him but asked him not to do any damage to the ship.

"We then," said Hewes, "were ordered by our commander to open the hatches and take out the chests of tea and throw them overboard, and we immediately proceeded to execute his orders; first cutting and splitting the chests with our tomahawks, so as thoroughly to expose them to the effects of the water. In about three hours from the time we went on board, we had thus broken open and thrown overboard every chest of tea on the ship. We were surrounded by British armed ships but no attempt was made to resist us."

They then — he said — went home, without having any conversation with each other or trying to find out who the other Indians were. There seemed to be an understanding that each man would keep his own secret and risk the consequences alone. Hewes says there was no disorder and that at the time people said it was the stillest night Boston had enjoyed for many months. However, there were a few episodes that do not seem to have been exactly orderly. While the tea was being thrown overboard, some of the citizens of Boston and of other towns tried to carry off small quantities of it for their own use. One man came on board and, thinking he was not noticed, filled his pockets and the lining of his coat.

Hewes was told by his commander to seize the man but only got hold of the tail of his coat, which tore off as its owner jumped from the vessel to the wharf. The man then had to run the gauntlet of the crowd on the wharf, receiving hits or kicks as he passed through. The next day the coattail, labeled with its owner's name, was nailed to the whipping post in Charlestown where he lived.

The Indians were determined that no one should get any personal advantage from the destruction of the tea. If the people of Boston had taken it and used it, they would have been thieves, not patriots. The next morning there was still a great quantity of tea floating around on the surface of the harbor. A number of citizens got into small boats and rowed around, beating the tea down with oars and paddles so that it became thoroughly drenched and impossible for anyone to use.

A small amount of tea came back to Brookline, for there were Brookline men among the Indians. It had fallen into the boots of one of the men who threw the chests overboard. It was not used but was kept for years, a dusty souvenir of the Boston Tea Party.

The fact that the night of the tea party was considered a quiet one gives us some idea what other nights must have been like. No doubt there was plenty of howling under Tory windows. There were frequent clashes between the members of the British garrison and the citizens. At last, on March 5, 1770, came the Boston Massacre.

Massacre is rather a large name for a street fight. It suggests thousands of peaceful men, women, and children butchered in cold blood by cruel tyrants. Actually, as it says under Paul Revere's engraving of the scene, "The unhappy sufferers were Mess[s] Sam[l] Gray, Sam[l] Maverick, Jam[s] Caldwell, Crispus Attucks, & Pat[k] Carr killed, six wounded two of them (Christ[r] Monk & John Clark) mortally."

Governor Hutchinson came to the scene of the shooting

and ordered the mob to go home, telling them that the soldiers and their officer, Captain Preston, would be tried. John Goddard was one of the witnesses at the trial. He had come in from his farm in Brookline with vegetables for sale. He was at the barracks on Water Street selling some potatoes when he saw about twenty soldiers with clubs "coming out of the barracks, seemingly much enraged." There had been an encounter earlier, he said, between the citizens and the soldiers near the rope walk. He added that one of the soldiers "swore in a very profane manner that he would be revenged if he fired the town."

It is undoubtedly true that the soldiers shot and killed unarmed men. Probably because their patience had been provoked many times by the patriots, they were acquitted of the deaths of the Americans killed that day. Probably the verdict was just. Yet as you walk up State Street and wait for automobiles to pass between you and the Old State House where George III's lion and unicorn are still in place, it gives you a strange feeling to see in the pavement the mark that shows where Crispus Attucks, a Negro, and other Americans died. You remember that they believed in liberty and the scuffle in the narrow street becomes important.

Paul Revere's engraving of what he called The Bloody Massacre in King Street was made from a crudely drawn picture. The work was hastily done. You can hardly believe that the craftsman who made the Liberty Bowl could have done such a poor job. Still, it shows how people in Boston and Brookline and other towns felt about the British garrison. The soldiers were angry, perhaps justly so. The picture makes us sure that the artist and the engraver were angry too. Perhaps the remarkable thing is that the colonists were patient so long.

I suppose Brookline has been getting smaller and smaller all the time you have been telling us about it," Susie said one evening.

She and her grandmother were making a model of a seventeenth-century kitchen and Andrew was building an aircraft carrier. His corner of the room was fairly neat because he was putting the carrier together out of a package. The other workers had a good many chips and shavings around. They were sandpapering the rungs for some seventeenth-century chairs. Susie dropped one and it disappeared.

"It's easier to make a new one than to hunt for it," her grandmother said.

Yes — she went on — Brookline has certainly shrunk while we have been talking about it. The wide paved streets have been turning into narrow muddy roads with logs laid across them in boggy places. In some, there are no roads at all but only footpaths through dark woods.

Churches, shops, and fire houses have vanished. However, the Punch Bowl Tavern exists already in the early eighteenth century. It is much smaller of course than we found it a hundred years later. It began as a sturdily built square hip-roofed house, painted yellow. Its rafters were cedar posts with the bark left on. We don't really know much about how it looked inside but we can be pretty sure that it had a big comfortable kitchen like the one we are making.

The Punch Bowl sign must have been a welcome sight as travelers came into the village. A tavern was a real necessity then. No one could travel far without stopping at one any more than you can now without stopping at a filling station. Horses had to be fed and watered and rested. Their riders had to eat and rest too. When they reached the Punch Bowl on a cold winter day, they were sure of a good fire, a hot drink for themselves, and "refreshment" for their horses.

There was no town hall in Brookline for many years. The selectmen had their meetings at the Punch Bowl and had their annual supper there. No doubt it was good. We have no record of what they ate but we do know the kinds of things that were being eaten at that time. For breakfast there might be rye bread, fresh butter, buckwheat cakes with maple sugar, broiled fish or ham, and of course pie. As soon as the weather was cold enough pies were made in large batches and frozen. They were thawed out when they were needed.

"I didn't suppose they had deep freezes!" said Andrew. "I thought they were a new idea!"

"The idea is an old one. It's working it by electricity that's new," his grandmother told him.

There was always — she added — a storeroom "out back" in these old houses where, as my grandmother used to say, it was "cold enough to freeze Injuns." Once frozen, a pie or a cake stayed hard a long time. When people went on a journey by ox wagon, they would take frozen cakes of baked beans and frozen brown bread with them. At dinnertime they would make a fire, put a little snow in a kettle, and the beans and bread. Pretty soon they would have a hot dinner.

Even the big fireplaces of the time threw very little heat into the rooms. Most of the heat went up the wide chimneys along with the smoke. That's why I made the settle to go next to our miniature fireplace. The settle kept off drafts and was much the warmest place to sit. Sometimes in an old house where the floor has never been painted, you can see a half circle around the fireplace that is a different shade of brown from the rest of the floor. An old man who had lived in a house like that in Vermont when he was a boy told me that the frost would lie thick on the part of the floor beyond the circle of warmth from the fire. This layer of frost had frozen and melted so many times that the color of the floor had changed. He said they used to hang their venison in the corner of the room after it had been frozen hard outdoors and that it would keep hard until they sawed off a piece and cooked it.

Game was still plentiful in those early days in Brookline. In the marshes there were great flocks of wild ducks and geese. There were bevies of quail and coveys of partridges in the woods. Sometimes passenger pigeons came over in great flocks. The sound of their wings was like a great rushing wind. If they lighted on trees, they could be knocked down with a stick and there would be pigeon pie for dinner. They were beautiful, but stupid birds and the people who killed them were stupid too. Now the birds are all gone. There were deer in Brookline woods and sometimes wild turkeys. Sometimes bear meat would be brought into town from farther west on the Sherburne Trail. The frontier had moved west but in Brookline people were not dependent entirely on their guns for meat. They raised their own pork and some beef, most of which they dried or pickled or smoked. Dried beef sizzled in butter with plenty of cream poured into the pan would often appear at breakfast or supper. At dinner there would be a big piece of boiled corned beef, put on the biggest pewter platter and surrounded by different vegetables — carrots, onions, beets, cabbage, turnips, potatoes.

The mother of the family always hoped there would be some left over so she could make hash for breakfast the next morning but she was usually disappointed. Bacon was not used often at that time but there were hams smoked with corncobs. Corn usually appeared in some form at most meals. It might be white corn meal made into jonnycake, hominy or samp, hasty pudding or Indian pudding, or young corn on the cob. Incidentally, Rhode Islanders, who have the best white corn meal, never spell it johnny. Another name for it was journey cake.

Jonnycake was baked on an oak board in front of the fire. The meal was scalded first, thinned with a little rich milk and spread evenly on the board. The board was propped up and tipped at the right angle to the fire. Some small boy or girl was given the job of watching the jonnycake. From time to time he had to lay the board flat and spread the steaming mixture carefully with a small amount of very thick sweet cream. When the cake was beautifully glazed brown on one side, it had to be turned and baked on the other. Turning the jonnycake without breaking it took great skill and had to be done by an old, experienced pair of hands.

Watching the toaster was another job that kept the children pleasantly warm in cold weather. The backlog in one of the big fireplaces might be five feet long and more than a foot thick. A good backlog would burn steadily for a whole day or even longer. In front of it were the foresticks, smaller and drier pieces of wood, which would burn down and make hot coals. When there was a good red glow just back of the andirons, they began to make toast.

"On a stick?" asked Andrew.

"There were probably people who used sticks or toasting forks," his grandmother said, "but if you lived near a blacksmith, he would make you a toaster out of iron.

"It has a long handle so that you can move it back and

forth — toward the fire and away again without scorching your face. The rack in front holds two pieces of bread and you can spin it around, so that as soon as the toast is brown on one side you turn it and do the other. With two toasters and a good bed of coals, you can make four slices of toast in less time than it takes to tell about. Each slice comes out with a white pattern on it that shows what the iron curves of the rack are like because of course the open spaces brown first. No two racks are exactly alike so each stamps a sort of trade mark on its product."

After people finished making their toast this way — she added — they put some more foresticks on the fire. Hanging on the crane there would probably be a kettle with something cooking in it or keeping hot. It might be a ham boiling or perhaps it was just hot water to wash the pewter plates and bowls and mugs. Not everyone at the table had pewter plates. Wooden trenchers were still used by the children. Sometimes in a big family there was a long, narrow wooden trencher that ran along the middle of a narrow table for all the children to use. The mother of the family would put as many portions in the trencher as there were children — for each perhaps some potato, some creamed salt codfish, salt pork cracklings, little new beets and beet greens — and then they'd all go to work with their pewter spoons. If one boy didn't want all of his portion, his brother would eat it. In fact the small ones probably had to work pretty fast to be sure they got their share.

The father and mother of the family, and any guests, had their food served on pewter plates that came from

England. You could turn them over and see a crown and a rose stamped on the back. The pewter was kept well polished with fine sand. Floors at this time were more likely to be sanded than to have carpets, especially in taverns. It was a good deal easier to sweep away the sand and put down fresh than it was to wash muddy footprints off boards or to clean rugs. Probably the Punch Bowl had a sanded floor and I think we'd better sand the floor of our kitchen when we get it made. What do you say, Susie?

Susie agreed that this was a good idea. She wanted to know if the Punch Bowl was the only tavern in Brookline.

For a long time it was, her grandmother said, but we know about at least two others. One was the Richards Tavern, which was near the corner of Heath Street and the Worcester Turnpike. Teamsters on their way to Boston stopped there. Stagecoaches rumbled past on their way to Worcester. Sleigh bells rang past it in the wintertime. At night you might hear the sound of fiddles and the tap of dancing feet.

The building was not always a tavern. It once belonged to the Winchester family and a remarkable preacher called Elhanan Winchester was born there. Elhanan could read any English book easily when he was only five years old. He studied the Bible and had an astonishing knowledge of it. When he was still very young, he could read Latin, French, Greek, and Hebrew. He had an amazing memory. Once when he was sitting in the gallery of the meetinghouse, his father noticed that the small boy was looking around him, apparently more interested in the building than the sermon. When they reached home, Mr. Winchester said that he was sorry to see that his son had been inattentive to what the minister said. Elhanan then proceeded to tell him not only the text of the sermon and where it could be found in the Bible but went on and repeated a great deal of what the minister had said.

"And now, father," the boy added, "if you will not be offended, I will tell you the number of people, the number of beams, posts, braces, rafters, and panes of glass in the meeting house. I counted them all and remembered the text too."

"What did his father say?" asked Susie. "Wasn't he pleased?"

"According to Miss Woods, who tells the story," her grandmother said, "his father 'with difficulty repressed a smile, but, assuming a look of gravity, he warned the child to give hereafter undivided attention to religious exercises when in a place of worship.'"

"I think that was mean, Grandma. Don't you?"

"No," said her grandmother, "just colonial."

Another old Brookline tavern — she went on — was the Dana Tavern. It was a big gambrel-roofed house with a row of sheds and outbuildings behind it. It started on Washington Street and ran almost to Harvard Street. It was less fashionable than the Punch Bowl or the Richards Tavern, probably because there was no ballroom. Most of its customers were the country marketmen who baited their horses there on the way to Boston.

If you had to spend a night in a New England tavern you probably were in for an uncomfortable experience. The chief trouble would be with the bed, which was not at all likely to be either warm, clean, or comfortable. If you read the wills of the time, you will find that the most valuable piece of household equipment was the bed and the bed furniture. This meant the bedstead with its high posts, sometimes plain, sometimes finely carved, its mattresses and pillows of goose feathers, its linen sheets, coarse but shiningly white, its homespun blankets of ivory-colored wool, and its embroidered valances and curtains and canopy that kept out the winter drafts. There was no spring. The mattress rested on ropes which also helped to keep the frame of the bed squarely in place. If the bed was very high from the floor, there would be a pair of steps to climb in by.

Getting into bed was an art in itself. If you were careless, the feather bed, as the mattress was called, might slip to one side and you would soon find yourself lying on the ropes. When the bed was made up, the feather bed was well shaken and the feathers were evenly spread around. However, they seemed to prefer to bunch up all in one place and there you were with your head in feathers and your feet on the ropes. The best way to do it was first to warm the bed with a pan full of hot coals, turn back the blankets and the upper sheet just far enough so as not to let out the warmth, and then dive into bed, pulling your feet in as rapidly as possible. A fine way if you were a talented high jumper. After that it was better not to move until morning.

Every now and then someone would kindheartedly warm a bed for a visitor and forget about the warming pan in the bed. Anyone who jumped into bed and met a brass warming pan full of hot coals usually jumped out

faster than he got in and not in silence. Of course the bed I've been talking about — all polished mahogany, clean sheets and soft feathers — was not the kind you found in a tavern bedroom. It was the best bed in a private house and often would be especially mentioned in a will and handed down to some favorite daughter. Dirty straw mattresses like the one Nathaniel Goddard slept on in Boston were much more common than feathers or even corn husks. People talk about the good old days, and there certainly were pleasant things about them, but anyone who wants the good old nights is more than welcome to them.

From Samuel Sewall's diary, we can get an idea of the kind of house that was being built in Brookline in the early part of the eighteenth century. Judge Sewall was a well-known citizen of Boston who also spent part of his time in Brookline because he owned land there. Because of his diary we probably know more about him than his friends and neighbors did. One day in 1702 he rode out to Muddy River, as Brookline was then called. It was still part of Boston and the houses were few and far between. We've talked about the town getting smaller as we've been traveling back through but it would be more correct to say that it has become emptier and in a way bigger because it took longer to travel through it and the woods were deeper and darker. There might even have been wolves in them, though it has been a long time since anyone has killed one.

Samuel Sewall's son had married a daughter of the Governor of Massachusetts, Governor Dudley. The parents of the young couple, both rich men, were planning to buy or build a house for them.

After his journey to Muddy River, Judge Sewall wrote to Governor Dudley, saying that he had "cheapened Devotion's homestead. He seems to offer it for £150." This is Judge Sewall's way of saying that he was trying to beat Goodman Devotion down on his price. Twelve acres of land belonged with the house, which was, he wrote, "raw and unfinished. There are two good lower rooms and one good chamber. That towards Bairstow's is but a sorry one, only you may see the windmill go in it."

"It sounds as if the windmill were in the bedroom. Did he mean you could see it from the window?" Andrew asked.

"Yes," his grandmother said. "The windmill was some distance away, across the field."

Judge Sewall — she went on — called the barn and outhousing of the Devotion place "ramshackled" and said the orchard was "much decayed." However, he said that the house "may be fitted up to accommodate our children. A new house will cost much money and then furniture and Stock for the land will be wanted. I am so far from having money to procure these things that I am already much in debt."

Governor Dudley was probably not much worried by this letter. Judge Sewall was one of the richest men in the colony. He had married Hannah Hull, the only daughter of John Hull, who was the mintmaster for Massachusetts. Hull's position gave him the right to stamp out all the coins used in the colony. The most famous coins John Hull made were shillings with a pine tree on them. The mint was such a profitable business that the mintmaster acquired a great estate including a large amount of land in Brookline. When the wedding of Hannah Hull and Samuel Sewall took place, Hannah's father gave her for her dowry her own weight in pine-tree shillings.

"I hope she was good and fat," Andrew said.

"It would be a nice present anyway," said Susie.

Her grandmother showed her a picture of a pine-tree shilling and said that even one of them would be worth having now.

"I wish I could find one," said Andrew.

At least you'd know what one looked like, his grandmother said, and went on to tell them that when the Mill Dam was built some workmen were taking down an old house in Brookline. The house was near St. Mary's Street on land that had once belonged to Judge Sewall and probably before him to John Hull. Back of the chimney they found quite a number of old coins. Among them were several queer black-looking shillings with a pine tree on them. They used them to pay their toll as they went back and forth across the Mill Dam to work. After a while someone noticed that there was something different about the coins and he offered to pay the workmen a large sum for them, but by that time all the pine-tree shillings had been used. Perhaps they had been part of Hannah Hull's dowry, but no one really knows where they came from or where they are now.

Sewall Avenue is named for the Sewall family. It was finally decided to built a house for young Sewall instead of trying to "cheapen" the Devotion house any further. Judge Sewall owned enough land in Muddy River for many houses — three hundred and fifty acres of it. It was land that had originally belonged to John Hull. It reached from Harvard Street to the Charles River and included much of Longwood.

Judge Sewall was famous not only for his wealth but also because he was one of the judges who condemned the Salem witches to death.

"Were there witches in Brookline?" asked Andrew.

"There weren't witches anywhere," said his grandmother. "There were some unfortunate women who were accused of being witches and condemned on evidence on which no one ought to send a rattlesnake to a reform school. I suppose there always will be people who like to believe the worst about their neighbors and feel important if they can tell strange stories about them. At least Judge Sewall realized that he had made a cruel and terrible mistake and confessed in public that he had done

wrong. Of course his being sorry could not bring the
dead people back to life, but at least it stopped him from
adding more cruelty and more victims to the list.

Judge Sewall, riding out toward Muddy River, probably never thought that his land there would sometime be
sold by the foot. He knew it was a good place to keep
cows and to cut salt-marsh hay for them. He might have
reached part of his own land by rowing up the Muddy
River in a boat. He certainly would have found it hard
to believe that anyone would ever ride across those
marshes on hard paved roads.

"When did Muddy River finally become Brookline?"
Andrew asked.

Not until 1705, his grandmother told him. Muddy
River, still part of Boston, had petitioned the General
Court in 1700 and again in 1704 to be made a separate
town. The petition was finally granted in 1705. Here is
a copy of it.

To his Excellency, the Governor, Council, and Assem-
bly in General Court convened. The humble petition of
the Inhabitants of Muddy River, sheweth:

That at a session of this honorable Court held at Boston
on 13 August, 1704, the said inhabitants exhibited their
humble petition praying, that the said Muddy River might
be allowed a separate village or peculiar, and be invested
with such powers and rights, as they may be enabled by
themselves to manage the general affairs of said place.
Which petition has been transmitted to the selectmen of
the Town of Boston, that they might consider the same;
since which your humble petitioners, not having been in-
formed of any objection made by the Town of Boston,

aforesaid, we presume, that there is no obstruction to our
humble request made in our petition.

Wherefore we humbly beseech your Excellency, that this
honorable Court will be pleased to pass an act for the
establishing of a separate village or peculiar with such
powers as aforesaid, and your petitioners shall ever pray.

Samuel Sewall Jr.	*Josiah Winchester*
Thos. Gardner	*John Devotion*
Benjamin White	*Joseph Gardner*
Thomas Stedman	*Thomas Stedman Jr.*
John Winchester	*John Ackers*
Samuel Aspinwall	*Josiah Stedman*
Eleazar Aspinwall	*Thomas Gardner Jr.*
William Sharp	*Ralph Shepard*
Edward Devotion	*Abraham Chamberlain*
Josiah Winchester Jr.	*Peter Boylston*
John Ellis	*John Ackers Jr.*
John Winchester Jr.	*William Ackers*
Thomas Woodward	*Benjamin White Jr.*
——— *Holland*	*Caleb Gardner*
——— *Gardner*	*John Seaver*
Joseph White	*Henry Winchester*

On the thirteenth day of November, 1705, the "prayer"
of these citizens of Muddy River was granted. Here is the
record:

"Anno Regni annae Reginae Quartae . . ."

"Excuse me, please — are you talking English?" asked
Andrew.

"Latin," said his grandmother. "It means in the fourth

year of Queen Anne's reign. The rest of it is in English.
It says:

At a Great and General Court for her Majesty's Province of
the Massachusetts Bay, In New England, begun and held
upon Wednesday, 13th May, 1705, and continued by several prorogations unto Wednesday, 24th October, following and then met 13th November 1705.

In *Council.*

The order passed by the Representatives upon the Petition of the inhabitants of Muddy River, a Hamlet of Boston, read on Saturday last,

Ordered, That the prayer of the petition be granted; and
the powers and privileges of a Township be given to the inhabitants of the lands commonly known by the name of
Muddy River, the town to be called BROOKLINE; who are
hereby enjoined to build a meetinghouse, and ordain an
able Orthodox minister, according to the direction of the
Law, to be settled amongst them within the space of three
years next coming.

Provided that all common lands belonging to the Town
of Boston, lying within the said bounds of Muddy River,
not disposed of, or allotted out, shall still remain to the
proprietors of said lands.

Which order, being again read, was concurred and con-
sented to.

JOSEPH DUDLEY
Taken from Mr. Addington's copy and sent to the Town.
A True Copy Examined by me.
ISAAC ADDINGTON, Secretary.
Recorded by me,
SAMUEL SEWALL, JR: Town Clerk

By these documents the people of Muddy River, a part of Boston, took their affairs into their own hands and became the people of Brookline."

"Do you know why they chose the name Brookline?" Susie asked.

"I know what my grandmother told me. She said that Muddy River was not considered a refined name, and that Brookline was only a more elegant way of saying that the Muddy River was the line that separated Boston and the new town."

Boston — she went on — was probably glad to get rid of the expenses of the poor little hamlet, fit only for a cow pasture, but it has tried more than once to get it back again. The people of Brookline have always treasured their independence and have managed to keep it. They found almost at once that managing their own affairs was an expensive matter. They were already paying a schoolmaster twelve pounds a year to teach their children reading and writing. Now they were supposed to build a meeting house, support a minister, and send a representative to the General Court.

People were beginning to clear more land for farms and they wanted something besides Indian trails leading to their house, so roads had to be built. Along the footpaths trees had to be cut down. If there was a rock in the way it had to be broken or pried loose. Unless, of course, it was one of the huge chunks of Roxbury pudding stone, in which case the easiest way was to do as Indians and cows had always done — go around. Some of these curves, one on Goddard Avenue for instance, are still in Brookline roads. If there were swampy places, they were filled in with stones and the logs that had been cut along the road were laid over them. Corduroy roads, they called them.

"Did you ever ride on one?" asked Andrew.

"Yes, and not so very long ago either," said his grandmother. "Like corded bedsteads and baked beans and pewter bowls, they lasted a long time and people kept right on using them. When your mother was a little girl there was still an old road in Brookline that had never been improved. It was called the Two Mile Road and it ran from Heath Street in Chestnut Hill through a piece of woodland that had belonged to my grandfather and then across Newton Street in the direction of West Roxbury. I rode over it on a horse many times when I was a girl and when your mother and uncle were little, I drove them over it in a Model T Ford. It never changed much in my memory of it and my mother remembered it about as I knew it. The wet places were corduroy. Although it was rather bumpy, I don't think it was any worse driving than on a washboarded gravel road or a hard-top road full of frost holes. I never was on the Roxbury side of it, just on the part that went through our own woods, but I think it was about the same kind of road."

It is hard-topped now — she went on — and you go along a piece of it to get to the new town incinerator, but up to a few years ago it was still just a narrow stony dirt road running through a wild piece of woodland. The swamps were full of pitcher plants and the wild azalea called Rhodora grew there. Even after they had been frightened away from the rest of the town, scarlet tanagers nested there. Spring peepers rang their silver sleigh bells there on April evenings and thrushes sang in summer. There were ruffed grouse all through the woods. Once your uncle jumped over a log and a mother grouse flying up from under his feet almost knocked him down. The nest was just a twist of brown oak leaves beside the log. It had fourteen bluish-green eggs in them. Nearby was Lost Pond.

"Why was it called that? Who lost it?" the children asked.

Their grandmother told them that she supposed the pond got its name because it was so hard to find.

If you wanted to go back into the seventeenth century and see what Brookline was like — she went on — you could just go and look for Lost Pond. On all sides of it there was a swamp — a colonial swamp for all you could tell. Marshy plants grew out of the wonderful black dirt. There was only one path to the pond. If you missed it, you would soon be up to your knees in mud. Trees and bushes were so thick along the path and around the pond that you couldn't see even a gleam of water until you got close to the edge. You couldn't ride your horse to the pond. You had to tie him to a tree and leave him among the skunk cabbages while you went on jumping across mudholes from one grassy tussock to the next. More than once, after half an hour of tussock jumping, I found I had missed the trail and finally got back to my horse never having seen the pond at all.

"What was it like when you did find it?" they wanted to know.

Just a round quiet sheet of water — she told them. It was so deeply shaded by trees that it was usually a silvery green instead of blue. Some of the trees around it were chestnuts with their sharply notched leaves and burs like green porcupines. In the autumn the chestnut leaves turned a wonderful bright gold and the oaks among them bronze and deep red. Close to the pond were swamp maples — the kind that turn scarlet and crimson and plum color, all on the same leaf. In wintertime when the ground was hard and the trees were bare, the pond was easier to find than at other seasons. I remember once coming on it sooner than I expected and seeing a pair of wonderful skaters waltzing there. The pond seemed like a secret ballroom with a silver floor and the walls hung with dark tapestries. The ballroom had a lamp because the full moon was just coming up above the trees. I never put my skates on but just stood there, watching the skaters whirling, dipping, and gliding until my feet almost froze. Then I went away through the dark woods. For a while I could still hear the music of the skates ringing on the ice but as I came out on the Two Mile Road again, I thought I must have dreamed that the waltzers were there.

Most of that swamp land has been drained now. They are building houses where the ferns and the Solomon's seal and the Jack-in-the-Pulpits used to grow. Swamps look the same as they did in colonial times but roadsides have changed. A great many of what we think of as the

commonest flowers came from England, probably as
seeds among loads of hay used on ships to feed animals
being imported. Hawkweed, daisies, buttercups, clover,
Bouncing Bets were all immigrants as much as John
Howland or Miles Standish. Or starlings or English
sparrows.

Ox teams were busy not just in Brookline but in all the
colonies widening and smoothing roads at the beginning
of the eighteenth century. Transportation was so much
improved that after a while it took only three weeks for a
letter to get from Boston to Philadelphia. In Brookline
more important than even the roads was the building of
the first meetinghouse. The town had promised that by
1708 it would build a meetinghouse and support a minister. It had to do these things in order to be considered
a town. However, the inhabitants of Brookline were so
few in number and so poor that they could not keep their
promise until 1715.

A piece of land was given for the meetinghouse by
Caleb Gardner, Jr. The land was on Walnut Street near
where the Unitarian parsonage now stands. Walnut
Street was still the Sherburne Trail, narrow and thickly
wooded on both sides. Neither Cypress nor Boylston
Street was even thought of. The committee for building
the meetinghouse consisted of Thomas Gardner, Samuel
Aspinwall, Erosamond Drew, Thomas Stedman, and
John Seaver. That odd name Erosamond belonged to the
owner of the only sawmill for miles around. It was somewhere in the region of the Two Mile Road. The water

power for it came from a brook that ran out of Hammond's Pond.

It had been voted by the town to make the building the
same size as the meetinghouse in Roxbury where John
Eliot used to preach and where the inhabitants of Muddy
River were part of the congregation. The Brookline
meetinghouse built by Samuel Clark was forty-four feet
long and thirty-five feet wide. There were at first only
fourteen pews. The rest of the congregation sat on long
benches. Around three sides of the building ran a gallery
where the children sat on benches. When they wriggled,
because the benches grew hard during long sermons, they
were rapped on the head by the tithing man. Later fourteen more pews were added on the floor and four were
built in the gallery. There was no steeple on this first
meetinghouse until 1771. When it was added, Nicholas
Boylston gave a bell, which was hung in it. There was
no clock. Time was measured by an hourglass kept on the
oak pulpit.

The building stood with its side to the road. When the
steeple was built, it was placed at the west end of the
church over the center door. The windows were dia-
mond-shaped panes of glass brought from England. Inside, the seats were arranged by a member of the town
appointed at Town Meeting. In arranging the seats careful attention was paid to the dignity, age, wealth, and
social standing of the members of the congregation.

In an old Brookline house, torn down in 1809, was
found between the floors a list showing how sixty-six

members of the congregation were seated in 1719. The
men and women were on different sides of the church
both downstairs and in the gallery. In the men's fore
seat were placed Josiah Winchester, Captain Aspinwall,
Joseph Gardner, and Edward Devotion. In the women's
fore seat were the wife of Josiah Winchester, Sr., the
widow Ackers, the wife of Joseph Gardner, and the wife
of Edward Devotion. Less venerable citizens and their
wives sat farther back. Younger Gardners, Winchesters,
Boylstons, and their wives sat in the gallery arranged
from front to back as carefully as earls and dukes at a
coronation.

The year that Brookline built its meetinghouse it did
not send any representative to the General Court of Massachusetts as it had a right to do. Instead the selectmen
sent an apology saying that Brookline was "only a poor
little town" and could not afford both building the meetinghouse and sending a representative the same year.

There were many hardships in those early years of the
town's history but on the whole it was a peaceful time in
which the town grew steadily. One of the early problems was the question of fences. They were important
because unless hogs and cattle were fenced in, they would
destroy growing crops. Fence viewers were important
officials elected every year. It was a question whether
animals should be fenced in or fenced out: that is,
whether the man who owned the hogs or cows had to
keep his stock from going into other people's gardens or
whether the man who owned the garden must fence it
carefully and keep the hogs out of it. In 1737, for in-

stance, it was voted that hogs should be allowed to go at large. So along any of the Brookline roads you might meet some hairy, fierce-looking old boar and if someone left the gate of the vegetable garden open, he was likely to have visitors who rooted out young carrots with their snouts and trampled down the beans. No doubt cows got into the corn and oats. As more crops were planted, the laws were changed. Cattle were allowed to graze along the roadside but only with someone in charge. This was usually a small boy. A good many fine Brookline citizens began their careers by being swineherds or cowherds.

In the new town of Brookline in the eighteenth century the wilderness was remembered but it had moved back. It was hard work to feed and clothe a family but it could be done without a gun by your side. The expenses of the town were heavy — thirty pounds in 1719 — but the town had its meetinghouse, its children could learn to read and write without tramping to school across the Neck into Boston. Cattle did well on the salt marsh hay. Erosamond Drew's sawmill was busy cutting boards for new houses.

The chimneys of these houses were so large that the foundations for them almost filled the cellars. A chimney with three stacks would contain enough bricks to build a modern house. More bricks too might be needed for the outside walls but unpainted wood was more common. The timbers and floors were of solid oak or roughly hewn by hand. One of these old houses was taken down after two hundred years and the beams were in such good condition that they were used again for at least another century. The inside walls of the rooms were paneled: wide clear pine boards without knots. Sometimes the pine was painted but sometimes it was left to mellow to its own soft brown.

To save space in these houses, they often had what were called turn-up beds in seventeenth- and early eighteenth-century houses. When the bed was turned up and folded back into a recess just big enough to hold it, it was concealed by a paneled door. Another space-saving plan was to have deep seats with hinged covers under the windows so that they could be used for chests as well as for seats. The fireplaces often showed bare bricks but in the keeping room, as the best room was often called, the fireplace was sometimes bordered with blue and white tiles from Holland. Or the designs were flowers and fruit or pictures illustrating Bible stories.

To get into the second story of such a house, it was necessary to open a trap door in the ceiling and pull down a ladder. In one of these old houses, originally belonging in the Gardner family, there was a secret room. When it was found in the nineteenth century, it had been forgotten for a hundred years or more. No one living remembered even hearing about the sliding panel in the ceiling that was the opening for it. It was completely dark and contained nothing but an ancient sword. On the hilt was a coat of arms which may have belonged to the Gardner family in England. Probably in the troubled days of the Indian Wars, and a hundred years later during the Revolution, the room was used to hide anything the family treasured. John Goddard, the wagon master, left his farm on Goddard Avenue in his old age and ended his days in this house, which stood near his son Benjamin's.

These seventeenth-century houses with the diamond-paned windows are all gone from Brookline now. Many of them might still be standing if they had not burned down or if they had not been taken down to make way for new buildings.

THE PEOPLE of Muddy River had always been on good terms with their Indian neighbors. This piece of good fortune was due especially to the work of John Eliot. He was the settled minister at Roxbury from 1632 until the end of his long life in 1690. People from Muddy River went to meeting at Roxbury before they had a meeting-house of their own. On Sundays Eliot preached at Roxbury but much of his time was spent riding along forest trails to preach at Indian villages. The twenty tribes of Massachusetts Indians came to know and love this stout kindly man, who not only preached Christianity but practiced it. At that time most white men felt that it was all right to cheat Indians. If the Indians did not like being cheated, they could always be shot. Eliot, however, regarded the Indians as human beings. He saw that they lived under miserable conditions and he did what he could to make the conditions better. They trusted him

and many of them became Christians or — as many people called them — Praying Indians. Even the smallest
papooses liked to see John Eliot come riding up the trail
because they knew that he carried apples or nuts or small
toys for them in his leather saddlebags.

Eliot learned the Indian language from an Indian servant of his. There were no books to help him learn so he
wrote one himself, a grammar of the language — a sort
of Indian primer. It was printed on the Stephen Daye
Press in Cambridge.

"Is that the old printing press that Mother showed me
in the Historical Society in Montpelier?" Andrew asked.

"It's the very press," his grandmother told him.

Later — she went on — there were two presses at Harvard, the Stephen Daye Press and a new one. Probably
both were used in printing John Eliot's great work — the
whole Bible translated into the Indian tongue. This was
printed in 1660. The full title was *Mamusse Wunneetu-
panatamne UP-Biblum God, naneeswe Nukkone Testament kah wouk Wusken Testament.* The short name for
it, the one generally used, is the *Up-Biblum God.*

An Indian named James helped in setting up the type.
He became so skillful that he was known as James Printer.
Copies of the first edition of the *Up-Biblum God* are
very rare because many were burned or lost at the time of
King Philip's War.

In this war at least six hundred of the best men in New
England lost their lives. As many houses were leveled
to the ground by the Indians. Thirteen towns were en-

tirely destroyed. Many Praying Indians were killed in helping the white men. Perhaps the Indians to whom the Bible was given did not understand it very well, even in their own tongue, but they understood Eliot's true Christianity. They knew he was sincerely their friend and in the struggle with King Philip they were on Eliot's side. Eliot had founded Natick, a place far in the wilderness in the seventeenth century, as a town especially for Praying Indians. He had tried to convert King Philip himself to Christianity but that was an impossible task even for Eliot. When King Philip and his warriors were on the warpath, attacking and burning villages, killing men, carrying off women and children as captives, the white men of New England were angry and they would have killed any Indians, even Praying Indians, if it had not been for Eliot. The Indians knew that he had stood between them and the anger of the white men and they returned his goodness with goodness.

Cotton Mather said, "We had a tradition that the country would never perish as long as Eliot was alive."

Boston could always have been defended from Indian attack by fortifying the narrow neck that joined the city to the mainland but Muddy River was in more danger. When it was known that King Philip's Indians were on the warpath, the people of the little hamlet gathered at the garrison house, which was fort and storehouse for the town. It stood near where Walnut Street and Chestnut Street now come together, across from the eastern side of the graveyard. The house was strongly built of logs. The upper story projected over the lower one and the floor boards in the projecting part could be lifted up to make loopholes. If Indians tried to set the house on fire, the men could shoot through the loopholes and the women could pour boiling water down on the savages. There is no record of its having been attacked but there must have been many times when the people of Muddy River, walking to Roxbury through the woods to hear Eliot preach, wondered when the attack would come. It was a long walk. A few men had horses and their wives rode pillion behind them, holding their babies in their arms. But most of the congregation walked. The father of the family and the boys carried their long guns and watched for any movement in the woods. Even when the fear of Indians began to die away there was still a chance that there might be a stray wolf among the trees. A bounty for killing a wolf near the Sherburne Trail in Muddy River was collected in 1657 by Philip Curtis.

Still, the danger of Indian attacks was never far away as part of a letter from Lieutenant John Sharpe of Muddy River to his guardian, Thomas Meekins, shows.*

It is addressed as follows:

"This for Loving Master Thomas Meekins living at Hatfield. This deliver.

"Loving and most respected Master:

"My love is remembered to you and My Dame hoping you are well as I am at the writing hereof, blessed be God

* I have simplified John Sharpe's spelling. L. A. K.

for it. My wife desires to be remembered to you and My Dame, and we are yet in our habitation through God's mercy, but we are in expectation of the enemy every day if God be not more merciful to us.

"I have been out 7 weeks myself and if provisions had not grown short, we had followed the enemy into your borders and then I would have given you a visit if it had been possible, for I went out a volunteer under Captain Wadsworth of Milton, but he is called home to recruit about their own town, so I left off the desire at present.

There is many of our friends taken from us. Capt. Jonson of Roxbury was slain at Narragansett. and Will Lincoln died before his wound was cured; Philip Curtis was slain at a wigwam about Mendham, but we have lost but one man with us these wars . . . However it is to fare with us God knows and we desire to commit all our affairs to his hands.

"So having nothing else, desiring your prayers for us, I rest

"Your servant
"JOHN SHARPE"

"Muddy River. 8th of the first month, 1676."

Lieutenant Sharpe never saw his old master and "My Dame" again. On the eighteenth of April he and Captain Wadsworth were both killed in a fight with King Philip's Indians at Sudbury. On the old stone that marked the spot was cut an inscription that read: "Capt. Samuel Wadsworth of Milton, His Lieut. Sharp of Brookline, and twenty six other soldiers fighting for defence of their country were slain by the Indian Enemy, April 18, 1676, and lie buried in this place."

There was still Indian fighting going on in 1690 and Lieutenant Sharpe's son Robert took part in it. He married Sarah Williams of Roxbury, and before he left for the war he wrote the following paper, leaving his affairs in his father-in-law's hands.

"Know all men by these presents that, whereas I, Robert Sharpe of Muddy River in the county of Suffolk in New England being bound out to the war, and leaving some concerns behind me, do ordain and constitute my loving father, Steven Williams of Roxbury my lawful attorney to let out my lands and to take rents and to sell and dispose as if it were myself . . . for the time of one year after date hereof if I return not. In witness I have hereunto set my hand and affixed my seal, this 16 of April 1690.

ROBERT SHARP"

Like his father Robert Sharp "returned not." He died fighting in the Canadian wilderness. His heirs inherited land in what was called Gardner's Canada. This was later the town of Warwick, Massachusetts. The old name was given to it because land there and in other parts of northwestern Massachusetts was assigned to soldiers who served in the Canadian expedition. Ashburnham was part of this same tract and was called Dorchester-Canada.

Another man who lost his life in the Canada expedition was Captain Thomas Gardner, who served under Sir William Phipps in 1690. With Sir William Phipps also, when his troops took possession of Port Royal and all the seacoast as far as the Penobscot River, was another soldier from Muddy River, Captain Samuel Aspinwall. He returned safely from these dangers but many years later he was drowned in the Charles River in sight of his own Brookline farm. He was given a military funeral and his body was carried to the grave to the sound of muffled drums. The company of which he had been captain fired a volley over his grave.

No doubt in spite of Eliot's example there were people in Muddy River who regarded all Indians simply as ignorant savages. Yet all white men in New England learned a great deal from their Indian neighbors. They learned how to grow corn and fertilize it and how to cook it in various ways. They learned to take part in Indian council meetings where they soon found that the Indians listened courteously and often spoke sensibly. The colonists used the Indian shell money — wampum — as part of their currency. If a man from Muddy River was in Boston and wanted to cross to Charlestown by ferry, he paid his fare in wampum. From the Indians the white men learned to slip along rivers easily in canoes instead of tugging at the oars of clumsy English rowboats. Many secrets of hunting, trapping, and fishing were learned from the Indians. Many of the games that Muddy River boys played and that Brookline boys still play were Indian games.

Modern lacrosse, hockey, football, and basketball are all based on Indian games. Javelin throwing and shooting with the bow and arrow belong to many countries but were practiced with particular skill by the Indians. They played jackstones, blind-man's-buff, and tug-of-war. They wrestled and had great running and swimming races. Indian children slid downhill on flat boards turned up at the end. The idea of our present toboggans came from these boards. Snowshoes too, are, of course, of Indian origin.

If a boy from Muddy River visited the Indian village near Chestnut Hill Avenue, he would often find the Indian boys spinning tops. They were very skillful at keeping the top in motion, whipping it from time to time with a buckskin lash. Sometimes a boy could run around his wigwam before the top stopped spinning. Rolling hoops was another favorite sport.

The greatest game of all was football. One of the most wonderful sights of the seventeenth century must have been this game, which the Indians called Pasuckquakohowauog. They played it on any wide level space that was soft to the feet but they preferred an open sandy beach, such as Revere Beach. The ball was made sometimes of wood, later usually of deerskin, stuffed with hair, and was much smaller than the present football. The goals were sometimes a mile apart. One village would play against another. There might be three or four hundred men on a side and a game would sometimes last several days.

The players began by painting their faces as if for war but they hung up their weapons on trees as a sign of peace. Then, as William Wood wrote in his *New England's Prospect*, "they make a long scroll on the sand, over which they shake loving hands and with laughing hearts scuffle for victory. While the men play, the boys pipe and the women dance."

He says the ball was sometimes kicked into the air and sometimes rushed along by the crowd of men and that it was "most delight to . . . view their swift footmanship, their curious tossings of the ball, their flouncing into the water, their lubberlike wrestling."

After the game on the beach the players who won could have dressed themselves in valuable furs. The goals were hung with all kinds of treasures which became the property of the winners — belts of wampum, beaver skins, blankets, black otter skins.

Wood says that "it would exceed the belief of many to relate the worth of one goal."

Like wampum, beaver skins were part of seventeenth-century currency. They were sent to England in exchange for the manufactured goods the colony needed: glass for diamond-paned windows or scarlet broadcloth for a man's coat or lace for a lady's dress. It is a mistake to think of our Puritan ancestors as all dressed in black or gray or brown. Inventories of old estates show that New Englanders had clothes of many colors. There were laws against fine clothes but I am afraid they were enforced only when the wearer was of "mean condition or calling."

From portraits as well as from the inventories we learn that men as well as women wore brightly colored clothes. There were violet waistcoats and petticoats. Stockings were often blue and so were aprons. Men wore blue or green or red — or all three colors at once. Scarlet wool cloaks that made them look like Little Red Riding Hood were favorites with girls and were handed down in families from mother to daughter to granddaughter. Until the colonists started growing their own flax and wool and doing their own weaving, they were dressed in materials imported from England. Mohair, serge, camlet, fustian, satin, lace, cotton, linen-flowered silk, ribbons, velvet, and linsey-woolsey could all be bought in Boston shops. No doubt the housewives of Muddy River went about brewing and baking in what were called sad-colored clothes, practical colors like brown and gray, but on the Sabbath the best coats and sashes and hats would be brought out. There would not be new ones very often. Styles could change in London or Paris or even in Boston but in Muddy River once you had a new camlet cloak with a velvet collar or a suit of purple broadcloth, your neighbors would see it for many years. Children were dressed like their parents. Boys looked like little old men with their long-skirted coats and knee breeches. Girls had dresses just as stiff and hard to move about in as their mothers'. Clothes were made over as long as the material would hold together. A boy's green jerkin might be all that was left of his grandfather's wedding suit. His sister's dress might be constructed out of her great-aunt's claret-colored tamie petticoat and trimmed with pieces of velvet that had been brought from England twenty years before.

The New England sayings:

Eat it up
Wear it out
Make it do
And go without

were certainly practiced in Muddy River. In 1646 a shop
in Roxbury tempted its customers with red, green, and
yellow cotton, two kinds of wool — gray kersey and green
tamie, blue linen, and scarlet broadcloth. It is quite possible that some of these things were first used in the
Roxbury meetinghouse on Sundays and worked their way
around to the fore seat of the Brookline meetinghouse
seventy years later. Perhaps they may still be in existence
as part of a patchwork quilt or a rag rug. Muddy River
did not grow into the prosperous town of Brookline by
throwing things away.

Indians were just as fond of brightly colored clothes
as their white neighbors were. They trapped beaver and
exchanged the skins for coats and shirts as well as for
knives and fire arms. A portrait of Ninigret, one of the
Narragansett sachems, shows a small man wearing an Indian costume — headdress, necklace and belt of wampum — and an enormous pair of English leather boots.
Another sachem, bringing twenty fathoms of wampum as
a present, visited the Governor. In exchange for the
wampum and promises of peace and friendship, Governor
Winthrop gave him "a fair red coat." Sometimes the presents to the Indians were cooking kettles or cloth for coats.
Tobacco and food of various kinds were given to them.
One sachem got a coat of moose skin. For another, Gov-

ernor Winthrop had a suit made of English cloth.
In return the Indians sometimes entertained white travelers with boiled chestnuts and puddings made of boiled
corn meal and blackberries. This special treat was an imitation of English boiled puddings which had currants in
them.

Many of the sachems on their way to visit the Governor must have passed through Muddy River by way
of the Sherburne Trail. The place they went through
was hardly as big as one of their own Indian villages.
William Wood in his *New England's Prospect* describes
it in this way: "The inhabitants of Boston, for their en-
largement, have taken to themselves farm houses in a
place called Muddy River, two miles from their town,
where is good ground, large timber, and store of marsh
land and meadow. In this place they keep their swine and
other cattle in the summer, whilst corn is on the ground
at Boston; and bring them to town in winter."

"So the cows and pigs were summer people," Andrew
observed. "Nothing personal, of course," he added
hastily.

His grandmother took no notice of this quip and went
on to read them Wood's rhyme about the animals that
might be found in the New England wilderness and just
as likely to be found in Muddy River as any where else.

The Kingly Lion and the strong-arm'd Bear,
The large-limb'd Mooses with the tripping Deer;
Quill-darting Porcupines and Racoons be
Castled in the hollow of an aged tree;

The skipping squirrel and Rabbit, purblind Hare
Immured in the self same castle are
Lest red-eyed Ferret, wily Foxes should
Them undermine if rampired but with mould;
The grim-faced Ounce, and ravenous howling Wolf
Whose meagre paunch sucks like a Swallowing gulf:
Black glistening Otters and rich coated Beaver,
The civet-scented Musquash smelling ever . . .

Wood adds conscientiously: "Concerning lions, I will
not say I ever saw any myself, but some affirm that they
have seen a lion at Cape Ann, which is not above six
leagues from Boston; some being lost in the woods have
heard terrible roarings as made them aghast, which must
be lions, there being no other creature which used to roar,
saving bears, which have not such a terrible kind of
roaring."

Wood's lions were probably catamounts. The rest of
the animals probably really were in the woods beyond
Boston Neck when Wood wrote in 1675. Some of them
may still live in what is left of the woods around Lost
Pond — that is if I am right in thinking that a "civet-
scented musquash" is a skunk.

Wood noticed birds and fish too and wrote about "the
Humbird for some Queen's cage more fit . . . the swift-
winged Swallow . . . the harmonious Thrush . . . the
sea-shouldering Whale, the snuffling Grampus . . . the
luscious Lobster . . . the flouncing Salmon." However,
luscious lobster and salmon and venison steaks were not
food for every day then any more than they are now.

An old account says: "The ordinary food for breakfast and supper was bean porridge with bread and butter. The bread was brown bread made of rye and Indian meal. White bread was used only when guests were present. Baked pumpkins and milk composed a favorite dish. For dinner twice every week, Sundays and Thursdays, baked beans and baked Indian pudding. The pudding was served first. Saturdays salt fish, one day in every week salt pork, one day corned beef, and one day if possible, roast meat was the rule."

The baked beans and brown bread, the Indian pudding (how surprised an Indian sachem would be to find ice cream on it!), the salt codfish in cream or made into prickly fish balls, the corned beef made into hash have all stood the test of time and can still be found on tables in sight of the Muddy River.

The first entry in the Muddy River Records was in 1686. By this time the inhabitants of this cow pasture for Boston must have begun to settle down for permanent residence because they were troubled about their children's schooling. It was too far for children to walk through Roxbury and across Boston Neck to school in all kinds of weather. One thing that we can be sure of — then as now — is that Muddy River had a wide assortment of weather. Boston, though it was only two miles off across the tidal waters of the Back Bay, was a long journey if you had to wade through flooded meadows in spring and snowdrifts in winter.

So the people of Muddy River petitioned the Town of Boston for the right to have a school of their own and to support it. Boston agreed and the following order was passed:

"That henceforth the said Hamlet be free from Town Rates to Boston, they henceforth maintaining an able reading and writing master."

The people of the hamlet agreed to pay a schoolmaster £12 a year and to tax the parents of school-age children enough extra to support a master. However, poor people were not to pay this extra tax. Their children could go free. From the very first the town was determined that every child should have his chance to learn. This was the first step in the separation from Boston, but selectmen were still chosen at the Boston Town Meeting to manage the affairs of Muddy River.

A committee of three men was chosen by the citizens of Muddy River to decide where the center of the hamlet was so that the schoolhouse might be built there. The place fixed upon was the triangular piece of ground west of the present First Parish Church. The first schoolhouse was accordingly built there, a small wooden building which lasted until the brick schoolhouse was built there in 1793.

Supporting their own school made the inhabitants of Muddy River feel that independence of Boston in all their affairs would be a good thing. Their first petition asking for complete independence, to have their own selectmen, and to support a minister of their own choosing, was made in 1700 and gave great offense to the Boston authorities. A Boston town meeting was promptly called, the petition was debated, and denied. Boston taxes were again laid upon the town, although Boston did agree to pay for the schoolmaster of Muddy River. However, this arrangement did not last long and by the beginning of the eighteenth century the town had its independence and also its new name.

Suddenly — as suddenly as it had started — Susie and Andrew's visit came to an end. Their mother telephoned that everyone was out of quarantine and that she and Janet and Olivia were going to drive down for them the next day. It was Friday when she called. They would be back in their own school on Monday, she said. They were partly glad, partly sorry. The Brookline school had been wonderful and they had made friends whom they would miss. But then there were their old friends to see in Vermont and the black and white pony, Sparkle Plenty, and all the new kittens, and Laddie, Susie's cocker spaniel, and all the Bantams. They would be in time for the wild-flower competition and for the Memorial Day exercises and the Graduation. It was time to start fishing for trout in the brooks and to swim in the pond. There would be

bicycle rides and picnics and square dancing and music
by candlelight.

"But I wish we could have finished the model of the
old kitchen," Susie said. "And I wanted to go to the
Planetarium again and we don't really know how Muddy
River first started. Oh, dear . . ."

"We'll work on the kitchen this summer," her grandmother said.

"Anyway I have my carrier almost done," Andrew said.
"And I'll finish while you talk about what you were going
to tell us this evening."

There isn't much left to tell — his grandmother said.
We've seen Brookline shrink from the way it is today —
a busy prosperous suburb of a great city, a place called a
town but with more inhabitants than many cities have —
to a struggling little hamlet on the edge of the wilderness
where people were so poor that it was a sacrifice to pay a
schoolmaster twelve pounds a year. Muddy River seemed
a wild place when they needed a garrison house and when
the men of the hamlet were away fighting Indians. In
1630 it was wilder and lonelier still. There were no white
men living in Muddy River. There was only one living
on the peninsula called Shawmut or Trimountain. He
was the Reverend William Blackstone. Like many of the
early settlers of Massachusetts, he had left England because he did not like the practices of the Church of
England. He lived all alone on Beacon Hill near where
Pinckney Street now is. He had gardens and orchards
there and grew fine apples. He cleared fields for his

cattle and he is said to have ridden around his pasture land on a tame bull. Perhaps it was Mr. Blackstone riding on his bull who made the first paths that are the basis for Boston's crooked streets. They are usually said to have been based on cowpaths but no one really knows just how they began.

We do know why Governor Winthrop and the other early settlers of Boston chose to settle there rather than where they first landed across the Charles River in Charlestown. In Charlestown the water supply was bad. Over on Shawmut, they were told, there were good springs. So one day in the summer of 1631 a boat crossed over from Charlestown. Among the passengers was an eight-year-old girl called Anne Pollard. As the boat drew near the shore, Anne jumped from the bow and landed before anyone else, the first white woman to set foot on Boston soil. She wrote about that first visit when she was an old woman — she lived to be a hundred and five years old — remembering how it looked when she saw it as a girl.

It was, she said, "very uneven, abounding in small hollows and swamps, covered with blueberries and other bushes."

The Indians had burned it over some time earlier and there were only a few trees left standing. One was an elm, which grew to a great size and lived on into the nineteenth century. It was known as the Old Elm. The Bostonians used to hang pirates and other people they did not approve of from it.

The English first called the place Trimountain because of its three hills. These were much higher in the seventeenth century than they are in the twentieth. They named the hills Beacon Hill, Fort Hill, and Copp's Hill. Fort Hill was leveled long ago. Part of Copp's Hill was cut away in the nineteenth century and used to fill up a swampy place where the North Station stands now. Even Beacon Hill is much lower than it used to be when there was a beacon at the top of it which could be lighted at night for a signal fire in times of danger.

William Blackstone sold his land, the whole peninsula of Shawmut, except for six acres around his house, to Governor Winthrop and his company for thirty pounds. Later he left Boston entirely, saying that he did not like the Lords Brethren — he meant the Puritans — any better than he had liked the Lord Bishops in England. The new inhabitants of Shawmut had come to America because they wanted to worship in their own way but they did not tolerate other people's religious ideas. Mr. Blackstone went to Rhode Island where other people who did not enjoy Puritan severity and intolerance settled also. There he again cleared land and soon had gardens growing and the finest apples anywhere around.

The settlers on Shawmut may have decided on a name for their new home before they sailed from England. Many of them sailed from Boston in Lincolnshire, the town in the fen country in the shadow of the great gray church with the square-topped spire called Boston Stump. Perhaps the fens and marshes of the new place — there were plenty of them when the tide was low — may have reminded the Puritans of the old country. Still they would probably have called the place Boston even if they had happened to settle near Niagara Falls. Muddy River, however, was not named from any feeling of homesickness for England but because the sluggish stream that wound through the fens actually had about as much mud as water in it.

Edward Johnson wrote in his *Wonder Working Providence* that Boston was "all surrounded by the brinish flood," and adds that "hideous thickets on this place were such that wolves and bears nursed up their young from the sight of all beholders." Mr. Wood, in *New England's Prospect,* wrote less dramatically. He said: "The situation is pleasant, being a peninsula hemmed in on the south side by the Bay of Roxbury and on the north side by the Charles River. The marshes on the shore side being not a quarter of a mile over so that a little fencing will secure their cattle from wolves. The place being bare of woods, they are not troubled with those great annoyances: wolves, rattlesnakes, and mosquitoes."

Across the Back Bay in the woods of Muddy River, they probably had all three annoyances. There were Indians too, Indians who might be hostile. The first time Muddy River was mentioned by anyone, Governor Winthrop wrote in his diary that "notice being given of ten Sagamores and many Indians assembled in Muddy River, the Governor sent Captain Underhill with twenty musketeers to make discoveries but at Roxbury they heard they were broken up."

These Indians were probably encamped at their fort in the Great Swamp. Much of Longwood, those parts that were not primeval forest, was swampy ground.

Knolls rose out of the swamp here and there and on one of these the Indians had enclosed about an eighth of an acre of ground with palisades. It was surrounded by a ditch three feet deep. There was a three-foot parapet and a gateway on each side. Even as late as 1844 the fort was still in existence.

Indians fished in the waters of the Back Bay. Their canoes might be seen where in 1955 the swanboats float in the Public Garden. They paddled along the Muddy River till it became only a shallow trickle of water where hills, High Street Hill among them, began to rise out of the marshes. The white settlers of Shawmut soon began to use the river as a highway. On the hills of Muddy River there grew the timber that was needed to build houses for Boston and the firewood to warm them in the cold New

England winters. The twang of Indian bowstrings soon gave way to the ringing of axes and to the sound of scythes being sharpened to cut the marsh hay. The wolves no longer had those hideous thickets where they nursed up their young. Their howls and the screams of catamounts

gradually gave way to the lowing of cattle. The wilderness had started to move westward and its first inhabitants, the Indians and the wild animals, had begun to move with it.

The Indians and the white men could not live together. This was not because the Indians began by being unfriendly. They were helpful to the first settlers, giving them corn and showing them how to plant it. The white men too meant to be kind, only their idea of kindness was to make the Indians over. The English settlers wanted the Indians to give up the laws of their tribe, to give up their lives of hunting and fishing and football, and to be servants for the English at a shilling a day. White laborers got two shillings. The Indians did not want to live like white men. Their idea of a good life was different. The dark tangled woods of Muddy River suited them perfectly. Game could flourish there. The woods were so silent that any movement of a deer or a bear among leaves and twigs could be heard. Fish could swim and spawn freely in the river and in the brooks that flowed into it.

The white men needed sawmills — sawmills and gristmills that choked the streams. They made clearings for their crops. They cut down trees for timber for houses and ships. The tall trees needed for masts had to be hauled by oxen, so more trees had to be cut down to widen the narrow paths made by Indian feet. The sawing of trees into boards was a noisy business that frightened the game. The sawdust spoiled the streams for fishing.

Game was killed by the settlers, not always for food but because it damaged their crops and their poultry and their cattle. When the Indians, finding game and fish scarcer and scarcer, stole a lamb or a chicken, or a young roasting pig, they were severely punished. White men who stole from the Indians could generally think up a good excuse. Of course the best excuse was that they were white men. Neither race was all good or all bad. When the Indians were dying of smallpox, there were white men who nursed the savages even after their own people had deserted them. There was John Eliot riding eighteen miles and more a day, through swamps and wet woods, carrying food and bundles of clothes to his red-skinned friends and those presents for papooses in his saddlebags.

Yet where the white men were friendly, there was still no place for the Indians. Soon they were only occasional visitors to Muddy River. If, when Anne Pollard first stepped out on the bare peninsula of Shawmut and looked across the Back Bay to the wooded hills beyond, she had asked some wise man what such a place would be in fifty years, he would probably have told her there never would be anything there but wolves and Indians. In another fifty years it was a cow pasture and wood lot for Boston and no one thought it would ever be anything else. Next it was a town, a poor little town, that couldn't even afford to send a representative to the General Court. The wise men of Boston never thought it would be busy and prosperous. They never would have let it be independent if they had. Yet the tangled thickets disappeared.

Farms took their place. City folks in Boston thought Brookline would always be a farming town with pigs and

cows in the muddy streets. They were wrong again.
Cattle were not allowed to go at large. Market gardens
had become more important than livestock and Boston
people began to consider Brookline as a garden from
which they could always count on asparagus and early
peas and peaches. Always was too long a day. Rich merchants discovered that Brookline made a pleasant summer
resort. Soon flowers grew where vegetables had before.
The market gardeners, like the Indians and the catamounts, went west. So people, intelligent people, thought
Brookline would always be a pretty little village around
the Punch Bowl Tavern, itself surrounded by hills from
which rich merchants in fine houses could watch their
ships sail into Boston Harbor. As usual they were
mistaken.

Without their knowing it, changes were coming. The
Mill Dam was being pushed out across the marshes. It
wouldn't make much difference, people thought. Tolls
were expensive and no one would travel on it. Still people
did cross it — a few at first, then tens, then hundreds,
then thousands. The tidal waters of Back Bay vanished
entirely. The railroads came. The old taverns disappeared. Shops were built in the places where once the
cattle used to stop and drink. Suddenly the town was no
longer a summer resort. There were no longer carriages
along its shady streets. Automobiles took their place and
people drove miles away from Muddy River for their
vacations. They began calling the town a "bedroom for
Boston" and complaining that there were not enough
houses in it and no room for any more. Yet the big estates

began to shrink and new houses appeared.

These houses would have amazed the Devotions and Aspinwalls. They had no looms, no spinning wheels, no dye kettles, no strings of apples hanging from the beams to dry. If they still had fireplaces these held some birch logs bought in Vermont, six for a dollar and strictly for ornament. There were flowers on the mantelpiece instead of powder horns. If there was a cider jug in the room, it had been made into a lamp. Perhaps the thing that would surprise them most would be the way a lamp is lighted.

Suppose — she said to the children — you go around the house and see how many things there are that stop when we have a hurricane and the power goes off.

They raced through the house and came back saying: "Freezer, refrigerator, roaster, toaster, vacuum cleaner, grill, iron, lights, washing machine, dishwasher, mixer . . ."

"Why, you couldn't do anything!" said Susie.

"That's right, except go to bed. I still have blankets that aren't electric," her grandmother said.

"I guess you're old-fashioned," Susie said thoughtfully. "I think it's nice to be old-fashioned — you remember so many things," she added politely.

Her grandmother laughed and said: "That's what grandmothers are good for. You see, I remember things my grandmother told me. Her own memory went back to 1828 when she waited until it was time to race to the Jinitin Tree. She told me things her father remembered, some of which I've told you. So if you remember some of the things I've said twenty years from now and tell them to your children, they will be reaching back to the

Revolution two hundred years ago. And earlier really. That little Anne Pollard who jumped out of the boat onto the shore of Trimountain was ever so many times your great-great-aunt. You have to travel back a long way but you touch her memory too.

A grandmother — she went on — is a sort of bridge between one world and another, reaching both ways. See, here's the last thing we took out of the trunk — the book your great-great-grandfather, James Edgerly, helped to publish. *Muddy River and Brookline Records* it's called. It was in 1633 that the first bridge that touched both Boston and Muddy River was built and here's the entry from the old record.

"It is ordered that a sufficient cart bridge shall be made in some convenient place over Muddy River." The convenient place proved to be near where Pond Avenue meets Huntington Avenue. After the bridge was built it was no longer necessary to wade through the river to reach the pastures and the green fields and the great stands of timber. With their "sufficient cart bridge" built, the people of Muddy River were ready to march forward.

First Things in Brookline

1633   First bridge ordered.

1635   First Farm in Muddy River laid out by Bostonians for "our teacher Mr. John Cotton."

1637   First list of property owners in Muddy River.

1639   First carpenter (mentioned) in Muddy River: William Blanton.

First bricklayer (mentioned) in Muddy River: Leonard Buttles.

1640   First highway laid out through Muddy River to Cambridge.

1640   First overseers of fences appointed.

First bridge built.

1642   First selectmen mentioned. (Chosen in the Boston town meeting.)

First men appointed to lay out highways "through Boston lands at Muddy River."

1651   First constable for Muddy River: John Kenrick.

First surveyor of highways at Muddy River: Peter Aspinwall.

1655   First inspection of Muddy River boundaries by "perambulators."

1669   First time magistrates nominated by the inhabitants of Muddy River.

1669   First elections of County Treasurer, deputies of the General Court, and selectmen by the inhabitants of Muddy River.

1671   First medical care of the poor of the town.

1674   First tax on Muddy River for war purposes (£184 17s for cost of King Philip's War) .

1686   First motion for a school in Muddy River.

First time that Muddy River, still part of Boston, raises its own taxes for a school and roads.

1688   First time constables nominated by inhabitants of Muddy River.

1688   First destruction by fire of property in the town when "three Indian children being left alone in a wigwam at Muddy River, the wigwam fell on fire and burned them so that all died." (Samuel Sewall's Diary.)

1698   First time assessors elected by the inhabitants of Muddy River.

First mention of a gristmill in Muddy River.

1700   First petition to make Muddy River a district or hamlet separate from Boston.

1704   First paving of roads.

1705   First recognition of Muddy River as a separate town called BROOKLINE.

First Burying Place in Brookline voted (though not acquired until some years later) .

1705–6   March 4. First selectmen of Brookline chosen: Lt. Thomas Gardner, Samuel Aspinwall, John Winchester, Samuel Sewall, Jr.

1707   First town clerk chosen: Josiah Winchester.

1707   First town treasurer chosen: Samuel Sewall, Jr.

1709   First representative of the town sent to the General Court: John Winchester.

1710   First schoolmaster chosen: William Story.

1710   First land given for a meetinghouse by Caleb Gardner.

1712   First Brookline school built.

1714 First meetinghouse planned.

1715 First money raised for a meetinghouse.

1716 First minister chosen: James Allen.

1721 First inoculation against smallpox. (Dr. Zabdiel Boylston inoculated himself and two slaves.)

1726 First separation from Suffolk voted. (The town did not become part of Norfolk County until some years later.)

1744 First town appropriation for military purposes. (Twenty pounds for a town stock of ammunition.)

1759 First time that it was voted to mend the highways by a rate. (This vote was reconsidered and it was decided to mend them "as usual." In 1768 they were mended by a rate.)

First time that it was voted that "the swine be cloistered." (Up to this time it had been voted that they should "go at large.")

1771 First bell given to the town.

1772 First steeple for the meetinghouse voted.

1772 First Bill of Rights voted. First Committee of Correspondence voted to assert rights of the colony against Great Britain: William Hyslop, Isaac Gardner, Deacon Ebenezer Davis, Captain Benjamin White, Isaac Child, John Goddard, John Harris.

1773 First Brookline protest against the sale of the East India Company's tea.

1775 Jan. 1. First volunteer company of soldiers organized. First plans for isolating smallpox patients.

1776 First men enlisted for the Continental Army.

1780 First election for Governor and other officers of the Commonwealth of Massachusetts.

1783 First survey of the town since the Revolution shows 4416 acres.

1787   First firewards chosen: Colonel Aspinwall and Lieutenant Croft. (Firewards had as their badge of office a
staff five feet long, painted red, and headed with a bright
brass spire six inches long.)

1787   First fire engine kept in the Punch Bowl Village.

1788   First Presidential electors chosen.

1788   First smallpox hospital erected by Dr. Aspinwall on
his farm.

1800   First singing school.

1801   First provision made for caring for trees along public
highways.

1804   First vote that cattle and horses shall not go at large
in the town.

1806   First planting of trees ordered by the town — around
the new meetinghouse.

1807   First use of Worcester Turnpike.

1810   First clock, a gift to the new meetinghouse from John
Lucas.

1814   First petition to build the Mill Dam (later Beacon
Street) from Charles Street in Boston to Sewall's Point in
Brookline.

1814   First volunteers enrolled for War of 1812.

1825   First Town Hall (now Pierce Hall) dedicated with
prayer and sacred music.

1828   First opening of the Mill Dam to public travel with
a procession.

1828   First Brookline fire engine house built.

1828   First Baptist Church dedicated.

1829   First post office.

1833   First plans for snow removal from roads.

1837   First report on town's finances.

1841   First plans for a high school.

1843 First report urging better playgrounds for the town.

1844 First Congregational Church established.

1847 First railroad train runs to Brookline on April twenty-fourth.

1848 First use of Town Seal.

1849 First Episcopal Church society organized. (St. Paul's.)

1849 First telegraph lines.

1852 First Roman Catholic Church built.

1853 First street lamps in use.

1857 First public library. (First library in Massachusetts under a statute allowing towns to have libraries.)

1857 First appropriation for police protection.

1857 First schools for adults voted.

1857 First store built at Coolidge Corner.

1858 First plank sidewalks built.

1861 First discussion of preparations for the Civil War. April 20.

1867 First public sewer. (Village Brook.)

1869 First public water supply.

1876 First public health work in the hands of a physician.

1880 First Bell Telephone Co. poles allowed on streets.

1882 First purchase of a horse for a fire engine. (Longwood.)

1886 First organized social and health work. (Brookline Friendly Society.)

1896 First public bath house.

1909 First motorized fire engine.

1913 First planning board.

1915 First limited town meeting.

Brookline Trees

Daniel G. Lacy, one of Brookline's best-known and best-loved officials, was for many years the head of the street department. He was especially interested in the roadside trees of the town. There are more than 14,000 trees lining the streets of Brookline and among them he listed the following kinds:

ELMS: English, American, Chinese.

MAPLES: Norway, Sugar, Red, Sycamore, Silver.

LINDENS: American, European.

PLANES or SYCAMORES.

WILLOWS: many species.

LOCUSTS: Honey locust.

CATALPAS.

MULBERRIES: White.

OAKS: Red, Pin, Scarlet, White, Black, Swamp.

PINES: White. Cedars: Red.

TUPELOS.

SWEET GUMS.

CAROLINA COTTONWOODS.

OHIO BUCKEYES.

FLOWERING CHERRIES. FLOWERING CRABS.

HICKORIES.

HORSE CHESTNUTS.

WALNUTS.

BEECHES.

ASHES: Red, White, Mountain.

SPRUCE: Norway.

TULIP TREES.

GINGKOS.

POPLARS: Lombardy.

This is not a complete list but it gives an idea of the many kinds to be found.

Bibliography

Among the books and manuscripts read in preparation for this book were:

ATKINSON, *Edward.* Journal and Letters.

BOTKIN, *Benjamin Albert, Ed.* A treasury of New England Folklore. 1947.

Brookline Historical Society. Proceedings. (A long list of papers about Brookline read before the Society, many of which may be seen at the Public Library.)

CURTIS, *John Gould.* History of the Town of Brookline. 1933.

DEARBORN, *Nathaniel.* Boston Notions. 1630–1847.

FORBES, *Allan, Ed.* Taverns and Stagecoaches of New England. 1953.

FORBES, *Allan, Ed.* Other Indian events in New England. 1941.

GODDARD, *Benjamin.* Daily Occurrences. (Manuscript diaries in the Public Library.)

GODDARD, *Julia.* The History of Green Hill. 1911.

GODDARD, *Louisa.* Letters. Mrs. Benjamin Goddard to Mrs. Samuel Goddard. (Original letters in the Public Library.)
Brookline Trees

GODDARD, *Nathaniel.* A Boston Merchant. 1767–1853.

KENT, *Louise Andrews and Elizabeth Kent Tarshis.* In Good Old Colony Times. 1941.

LITTLE, *Nina Fletcher.* Some Old Brookline Houses. 1949.

Muddy River and Brookline Records. 1634–1838.

MUSSEY, *Barrows, Ed.* Old New England. 1946.

MUSSEY, *Barrows, Ed.* We Were New England. 1937.

WEEDEN, *William B.* Economic and Social History of New England. 1620–1789. 2 v.

WILDER, *David.* The History of Leominster. 1853.

WINSOR, *Justin, Ed.* Memorial History of Boston. 1880–82.

WOODS, *Harriet F.* Historical Sketches of Brookline, Massachusetts. 1874.

Statistics

1950
    Population, 57,589

    Town budget, $11,944,362.93

    Books in the Library, 205,681

    Teachers in the schools, 256

1895
    Town budget, $1,659,311.75

    Employees in Police Department, 72

    Employees in Fire Department, 84

    Population in 1900, 19,935

    Teachers in schools, 125

    Books in Library, 53,315

1835
    Budget in 1850, $11,595 (approx.)

    Policemen, 1

    Volunteer firemen in 1847, 37

    Population in 1850, 2,516

    Teachers in schools in 1834, 5

    Books in Library in 1857, 1000

1800   Budget $2600 (about)

Constables, 1

Population, 605

Books in Brookline Social Library, 400

1775   Volunteer fire company, 8 or 10 men

1730   Constables, 1

Budget, £300

Population in 1765, 338

1700   Town expenses — Money to keep up the
Pound for stray animals

£12 to pay a schoolmaster

Constables, 1

Population, about 50 families

Index

Printed in the United States
35378LVS00001B/46-204